Mihály Károlyi & István Bethlen

Mihály Károlyi & István Bethlen
Hungary
Bryan Cartledge

HAUS HISTORIES

First published in Great Britain in 2009 by
Haus Publishing Ltd
70 Cadogan Place
London SW1X 9AH
www.hauspublishing.com

A CIP catalogue record for this book
is available from the British Library

ISBN 978-1-905791-73-6

Series design by Susan Buchanan
Typeset in Sabon by MacGuru Ltd
Printed in Dubai by Oriental Press
Maps by Martin Lubikowski, ML Design, London

Contents

Prologue   vii

I Two Lives and the Land   1
1 Hungary's Thousand Years   3
2 Mihály Károlyi and István Bethlen   17
3 Collapse and Revolution   31
4 Prelude to Paris   43

II The Paris Peace Conference   53
5 Károlyi Abdicates   55
6 Dismemberment   67
7 Counter-revolution   81
8 Paris   91

III The Legacy   109
9 Bethlen – Consolidation and Recovery   111
10 Károlyi and Bethlen: Endgame   128

Epilogue   141
Notes   144
Chronology   150
Further Reading   164
Picture Sources   168
Index   171

In Parliament Square, Budapest, Count Mihály Károlyi proclaims the Hungarian Republic on 16 November 1918.

Prologue

Budapest, 8 June 1896. On a fine summer's day, the Hungarian capital was *en fête*. Franz Josef, Emperor of Austria and King of Hungary, was making one of his infrequent visits to his Kingdom and second capital. The Empress Elisabeth, a melancholy beauty known to prefer Hungary's open spaces and lively horses to the cold formality of the Hofburg, was at the Emperor's side, cheered with special warmth by the Hungarian crowds. Some 1,700 horsemen in traditional uniforms, representing all the county regiments and feudal militia of the nation, escorted their state coach from the Royal Palace to the Coronation Church of St Matthias, and thence across the Danube to the new gothic Parliament building. Even the correspondent of the London *Times*, down from Vienna for the occasion, was impressed:

'It would be a hopeless task to endeavour to give anything like a complete idea of the hundreds of uniforms and costumes of all the colours of the rainbow in a procession that took nearly two hours to cross the Danube. The 80 municipal and county bands presented numerous variations of Hussar uniforms, a number of peasant costumes, and various suits of chain mail, with battle-axes and loaded clubs. These costumes rang all sorts of changes on the polychromatic scale, from the sober tints favoured by the sturdy peasants ... to the most aggressive scarlet and sulphur yellow, azure and dazzling white, violet, purple, gold, rich crimson and ruby. There were innumerable leopard skins and panther fells slung over the shoulder with careless grace.'[1]

As the procession slowly wound its way down Castle Hill and across the Margaret Bridge, trumpet fanfares blared and cannon thundered salutes to the Monarch and his consort. When they were not admiring this pageant of Hungary's ruling class, the people of Budapest and their fellow Hungarians from throughout the kingdom could regale themselves at the mass picnic in Vérmező Park, where oxen roasted on spits, and from the myriad stalls in City Park. During the celebrations, 5,600 litres of wine and 32,000 pairs of sausages were consumed daily.

The Hungarian nation was celebrating its Millennium, 1,000 years of history since the occupation of the Carpathian basin by the Magyar tribal confederacy in the year AD 896. Two future Prime Ministers of Hungary rode in the procession, perspiring with their fellow nobles in full ceremonial dress: Count Mihály Károlyi, with the regiment of his native county, and Count István Bethlen, a law student at Budapest University, with the large Transylvanian contingent. They were both destined to play leading roles in the most disastrous series of events ever to befall their country; one of them would guide her towards recovery.

Count István Bethlen, Prime Minister of Hungary, in 1926.

I
Two Lives and the Land

1
Hungary's Thousand Years

The history of more fortunate nations is punctuated by triumphs and victories. The history of Hungary is punctuated by disasters and defeats. The Hungarian achievement is survival and recovery.

One hundred years after the Magyar tribes had occupied the fertile Carpathian basin and, for half a century, terrorised Europe in predatory raids which extended from Bremen to Bologna, King Stephen I laid the foundations of a Christian European kingdom. Although he displayed great military talent in defeating those who challenged his authority, Stephen I was above all a man of peace and order. He gave Hungary her Western orientation, embracing Catholicism rather than Orthodoxy, and an administrative structure of which the central feature, the county, has survived to this day. His political achievements fully justify the reverence that Hungarians still, a thousand years later, accord to his memory. The Holy Crown which Pope Sylvester II sent to Stephen for his coronation on Christmas Day in the year 1000 became, and remains, the prime symbol of Hungary's statehood. Stephen was canonised in 1083.

Stephen's legacy survived Hungary's first major disaster, the invasion in the 13th century by Mongol hordes which overran the country, sacked its towns and villages and decimated her population. Béla IV, one of the few competent rulers of the Árpád dynasty, rebuilt the kingdom, improved its defences, re-established the rule of law and bequeathed to the succeeding Anjou kings a viable state, respected by its neighbours and by now controlling not only the Carpathian basin but Croatia and the Dalmatian coast as well. Building on this inheritance, the Angevins made Hungary one of the most powerful states in Europe, uniting in the person of Louis the Great the Hungarian and Polish crowns and producing (by marriage) in Sigismund I her first Holy Roman Emperor. But Hungary's strength was more apparent than real. The extensive territories whose allegiance the Hungarian crown commanded far exceeded its capacity to control or defend them. Growing internal antagonisms – between crown and over-mighty barons, between over-privileged nobles and over-burdened peasants – together with a small population and an underdeveloped economy, imposed severe handicaps on Hungary's ability to hold her own, sandwiched as she was between the rising empires of Habsburg Austria to the north and the Ottoman Turks to the south. Not for the last time in Hungary's often tragic story, nemesis succeeded hubris: in 1526, on the field of Mohács, the invading Turks under Suleiman the Magnificent annihilated Louis II's army. Louis himself perished, together with the majority of Hungary's barons and nobility. Hungary lay prostrate, a battlefield over which the Turks and rival claimants to the Hungarian crown fought and pillaged.

For nearly two centuries Hungary, like Caesar's Gaul, was divided into three parts: a large central and southern zone occupied by the Turks, a north-western crescent ruled by the Austrian Habsburgs, who had won the struggle for the Hungarian crown and, to the east of the river Tisza, the autonomous principality of mountainous Transylvania where, under successive Hungarian rulers but under Turkish protection, the flame of Hungarian independence and the first shoots of Hungarian culture were kept alive. Transylvania became the base from which, during the 17th century, repeated attempts were launched, with or without Turkish sanction, to oust the alien Habsburgs and forge a united, independent Hungary. They all failed – but with honour and glimpses of eventual triumph. In the early 18th century Ferenc Rákóczi, who led a predominantly Protestant army in the eight-year War of Independence, fought the Austrians to a virtual draw but failed to oust them. Meanwhile, the defeat of the Turks before Vienna by the Austrians and Poles and the subsequent liberation of Buda (not yet united with Pest) had led in 1699 to the final expulsion of the Turks from Hungary – but also to the consolidation of Habsburg rule, which was to remain unchallenged for over a century.

The absence of an open challenge to the Habsburgs by no means implied that the Hungarians had lapsed into passive submission. The bicameral Diet (Parliament), through which since the early Middle Ages Hungary's noble ruling class – the magnates and the gentry – had expressed their views to the Crown and when necessary defended their interests against it, conducted, during the 18th century, a stubborn defence of the constitutional rights and privileges which successive Hungarian kings had been obliged to recognise. Of these, the most conspicuous and the most controversial was the exemption of the Hungarian nobility from taxation, which provided Habsburg rulers with a pretext to impose harshly

MAGYAR – THE LANGUAGE OF HUNGARIANS
The term 'Hungarian' embraces all inhabitants of the Hungarian state, including the 'nationalities' – Slovaks, Romanians, Serbs, Croats, Germans and Ruthenians. The term 'Magyar' relates to those Hungarians whose first language is Magyar and who think of themselves as descendants, however remote, of the original progenitors of the Hungarian nation. The impact of the Enlightenment on Hungary, from the mid-18th century onwards, inspired interest in and enthusiasm for the Hungarian language. Hungary's political and literary language, used by the educated classes for all purposes except informal conversation, was still Latin, a circumstance unique in Europe. Hungary's leading poets of the Enlightened era not only promoted the vernacular as a literary language but married that language to patriotism and a national ideal, thus planting the roots of nationalism. By the turn of the century, enthusiasm for the Hungarian language had begun to acquire nationalistic overtones; non-Hungarian speaking ethnic groups began to be held in contempt. The 'nationality question', which was to exert a malign influence on Hungarian political life for the next century and a half, had been born.

discriminatory tariffs on Hungarian exports to the rest of the Monarchy. The attempts of the Empress Maria Theresa and her son, Joseph II, both to oblige Hungarian nobles to contribute their share towards the defence of their kingdoms and to impose upon them badly-needed measures of social and economic reform generated tensions between Hungary and Vienna which made an eventual rupture probable if not inevitable. At the century's end, Hungary was still a feudal society whose backward rural economy depended in large part on the medieval institution of serfdom. It was also a heterogeneous society in which ethnic Hungarians – the Magyars – accounted for only 39 per cent of a population of 8.6 million; the growth in numbers of ethnic minorities, the so-called 'nationalities' – Slovaks, Romanians, Croats, Ruthenians, Serbs and Germans – created another potential source of tension alongside the economic deprivation and hardship of the countryside. The ideas of the Enlightenment had inspired a rapidly developing sense of Hungarian nationhood and patriotism.

Ominously, however, the influence of the Enlightenment was encouraging a sense of national identity and cultural pride among the 'nationalities' as well. Surrounded by Slavs, the Hungarians had always harboured a sense of being under threat from without; they now began to sense a mounting threat from within.

Economic backwardness and consequent vulnerability to the collapse of agricultural prices after the Napoleonic wars, together with increasing social tensions, persuaded the thinking members of Hungary's noble class – the writers, poets and political activists – that something had to be done. This imperative inspired, during the first half of the 19th century, the activities of a remarkable group of men – István Széchenyi, Lajos Kossuth and Ferenc Deák prominent among them – who during 'the age of reform' wrote the greatest pages of their country's history.

By the mid-1840s, their parliamentary work, their writing and their rhetoric had resulted in a torrent of measures of economic, social and administrative reform which dismantled the institutions of feudalism and established the essentials of a civil society. The experience of exercising more active control over Hungary's affairs in those areas of policy within its jurisdiction, together with the example of revolutionary movements elsewhere in Europe, encouraged the Hungarian Diet to challenge royal authority in areas traditionally reserved to the monarch's prerogative. Unnerved by open revolt on the streets of both Vienna and Pest in March, 1848, Emperor Ferdinand V reluctantly sanctioned a body of legislation, the 'April Laws', which completed Hungary's

ISTVÁN SZÉCHENYI (1791–1860)
Count István Széchenyi was born in 1791 into one of Hungary's most eminent magnate families. After a short but distinguished military career he became a dedicated traveller, driven by an intense and intelligent curiosity about the workings of countries other than his own. His visits to England gave him a profound admiration for English political institutions, social mobility and way of life. He agreed with Jeremy Bentham that old laws and customs, however hallowed, should be discarded if they were no longer useful – the dead should not exercise a tyranny over the living. He was no democrat, believing that 'the continued preponderance of the landowning classes [is] the sole guarantee for the survival of the nation'. But he also believed, passionately, in the urgent necessity for social and economic reform – gradual reform, by consensus – in Hungary. He argued that the landowner, as much as the peasant, was a prisoner and victim of the feudal system by which Hungary was still afflicted and directed his efforts to persuading his own class of this in three ground-breaking books, of which the best known is *Hitel* ('Credit'). Landowners, he urged, should be freed from the shackles of the law of entail which prevented them from obtaining credit for investment, since they could not offer their land as security. Széchenyi was no mere theoretician but a hands-on reformer: he helped to found and fund Hungary's Academy of Sciences, launched the project for a Chain Bridge to link Buda with Pest, introduced horse breeding and horse racing into Hungary and established Hungary's first English-style club in Pest. His life was clouded, however, by frequent and profound depressions which eventually eroded his sanity and led to his suicide in 1860. He nevertheless wholly merited the accolade bestowed upon him by his more radical rival and eventual opponent, Lajos Kossuth, who called him 'the greatest Hungarian', a primacy which remains unchallenged.

transformation from a backward, stagnant province of his Empire into a vital, reformed and all but independent state.

A few months later, the threat to his throne having passed and encouraged by the growing hostility of the 'nationalities', led by Croatia, towards the Hungarian Diet, Ferdinand revoked his sanction, encouraged the Croats to invade Hungary and made open war between Austria and Hungary inevitable. Between September 1848 and August 1849, the Hungarian National Defence Force raised by Kossuth defeated the Croats, fought the Austrians to a standstill and obliged the new Emperor, Franz Josef, to appeal for Russian help, which Tsar Nicholas I was only too ready to provide. The odds against Hungary's latest and greatest bid for independence now became overwhelming. Her surrender to the Russians was followed by a spasm of savage revenge by the Austrians which numbed defeated Hungary and shocked Europe. Once again, however, Hungarians demonstrated their remarkable resilience and capacity for recovery.

During the succeeding two decades, Hungary and Austria groped their way cautiously, and with frequent setbacks, towards the accommodation which both sides came to recognise as essential. Geography and their shared history had condemned the two countries to an unhappy marriage from which neither side could afford to seek divorce. Without Hungary, Austria could not be numbered among the Great Powers; without Austria, Hungary would be at their mercy. Under the terms of the 'Compromise' of 1867, Hungary became an independent and theoretically equal partner in a Dual Monarchy in return for agreeing to share with Austria responsibility for foreign affairs, defence and the expenses associated with those areas of policy. Bitter controversy over the terms of this bargain dominated Hungarian politics until 1914 and beyond. There were those, like Lajos Kossuth, now in exile, who believed that Hungary had given away too much and should have exploited Habsburg weakness – especially after Austria's defeat by Prussia in 1866 – to make a dash for full independence. The majority of Hungary's ruling class, however, agreed with Ferenc Deák, her leading statesman and negotiator of the 'Compromise', that retention of the existing constitutional structure, with a monarch – albeit Austrian – at its apex offered the best guarantee of social stability at a time when this was threatened by the rising aspirations of the non-Magyar 'nationalities' within the kingdom.

The 'Compromise' regained for Hungary the rights and privileges which, over three centuries, she had fought to preserve against Habsburg absolutism and, after 1849, neo-absolutism; it also consolidated the social and economic dominance of the Magyar landowning class. By 1896, when it paraded through Budapest (Buda and Pest had been united in 1872) to honour the King-Emperor and the Millennium, that class had much to celebrate. Thanks in large part to her large, energetic and talented Jewish community and to a mounting inflow of foreign capital, Hungary's economy, both agricultural and industrial, had advanced considerably since the 1850s. The large estates flourished under the protection of the customs union with Austria. Under Kálmán Tisza, the inappropriately named Liberal Party had dominated Hungarian politics for three decades, giving Hungary the stability which was essential to economic progress.

The triumphalism and pageantry of the Millennium and the sudden effulgence of Budapest as an elegant and modern European capital had tended to divert attention from the internal problems and tensions which, by 1914, had become so serious as to threaten the very integrity of the Hungarian state. The emancipation of the serfs in 1848, confirmed in 1853, had brought little relief to the rural population. The plots of which former serfs had become owners were typically too small to sustain a family; and over a third of the peasantry had no land at all, depending on seasonal and casual employment for survival. Even in the late 19th century, the threat of starvation still hung over the Hungarian countryside. Harvest strikes and outbreaks of violence by desperate peasants became commonplace and were brutally suppressed by the hated gendarmerie and sometimes by the army. Having no parliamentary representation through which to seek redress – only 6 per cent of the Hungarian population had the vote and until 1913 there was no secret ballot – emigration offered the only escape from destitution; between 1869 and 1910, 1.25 million Hungarians, mostly from the rural and urban proletariats, left for the United States and Western Europe.

Rural poverty exacerbated the discontent of the 'nationalities', most of whom lived in the least prosperous agricultural regions, around the fringes of the country. Slovaks, Romanians, Serbs and Croats, moreover, had been and continued to be subject to the cultural persecution dubbed 'Magyarisation' – policies designed by successive Magyar-dominated governments to ensure the supremacy of the Magyar language and with it Magyar control of the heterogeneous Hungarian state. Secondary schools and cultural institutions in predominantly non-Magyar regions were closed down and compulsory instruction in the Magyar language given pride of place in non-Magyar schools at all levels, from the kindergarten upwards. The relatively liberal Nationalities Act of 1868, intended to safeguard the rights of the national minorities, had been largely ignored by the local authorities whose duty it was to implement it; and the 'nationalities' had boycotted the parliamentary process in protest. The resulting tensions only rarely erupted into violence – the various political organisations which emerged among the 'nationalities' generally decided to bide their time; but serious riots in Croatia in 1903 inaugurated a decade during which relations between the Magyar ruling establishment and the 'nationalities' went from bad to worse. The disintegration of the Hungarian state awaited only a catalyst.

To make matters worse, Hungary laboured, during the first decade of the 20th century, under the handicap of a weak and incompetent coalition government which lasted until the electoral victory in 1910 of István Tisza – son of Kálmán – at the head of the newly formed Party of Work. First as Speaker of the Lower House of Parliament and then, from 1913, as Prime Minister Tisza cut through the tangle of constitutional wrangling in which the Austro-Hungarian relationship had become bogged down – and which had deprived the Monarchy of badly-needed defence funding – and restored working relations with Vienna; as a member of the Common Ministerial Council, the key policy-making body of the Dual Monarchy, Tisza gave Hungary a voice, for the first time since Count Gyula Andrassy's brilliant tenure as the Monarchy's Foreign Minister, in foreign policy – and this at a critical time. Tisza's policies stemmed from two core beliefs, to which he adhered with iron determination and sometimes with passion. The first was his belief in the sacred mission of the nobility to lead the Hungarian nation, preserving both its unity and its Magyar character; from this followed his resistance to any extension of the electoral franchise – only the Magyar landowning class could be trusted to exercise political rights to the benefit of the nation as a whole. Peasants were, he said, 'incapable of exercising their political rights, unreliable from the standpoint of national unity, enlightenment and human progress and easy targets for … demagogy'.[1] The second was his belief in the vital importance to Hungary of the Monarchy's alliance with Germany: 'It is the Hungarian nation that supports our [the Monarchy's] intimate alliance with the German Empire, more directly perhaps than even the

Austrian Germans. This is the cornerstone of our entire policy; we remain true to and proclaim the enduring principle … that the Hungarian nation must carry out its historic mission shoulder to shoulder with the great German nation in true political solidarity.'[2]

After the assassination of Archduke Franz Ferdinand and his wife in Sarajevo on 28 June 1914, Tisza argued passionately in the Ministerial Council against making the murders a pretext for war against Serbia, the course which Austrian ministers were urging on the Emperor. Tisza realised, and told Franz Josef directly, that 'an attack upon Serbia would conjure up war with Russia and thus world war'. In this, he showed a clearer vision than any of his European counterparts. But Tisza proved vulnerable to the argument that Kaiser Wilhelm, who favoured retaliation against the Serbs, would think less of Austria-Hungary if the Monarchy held back – he would interpret this as weakness and Hungary's interests would suffer as a result. True to his belief in the prime importance of the German alliance, Tisza reluctantly gave in and voted for war – an outcome duly secured by Vienna's delivery to Serbia, on 23 July 1914, of an ultimatum so framed as to ensure its rejection.

Had Tisza been superstitious, which he was not, he might have been impressed by the coincidence of the delivery of the ultimatum with the impact on Budapest of a freak tornado. Winds of over 100mph destroyed dozens of buildings, ripped the roof from St Stephen's Basilica, severely damaged the Coronation Church, closed the Chain Bridge and caused numerous casualties, some of them fatal.

Most Hungarians welcomed the opportunity to settle accounts with the insubordinate Southern Slavs. In Budapest, as in the capitals of the other eventual belligerents, the bands

Europe 1914

Petrograd (St Petersburg)

Riga

Moscow

Vilna

Königsberg

RUSSIAN EMPIRE

Warsaw

Brest-Litovsk

Kiev

Budapest

Odessa

ARY

ROMANIA

Black Sea

Belgrade   Bucharest

SERBIA   BULGARIA

RO   Sofia

ANIA

Constantinople

GREECE

OTTOMAN EMPIRE

Athens

played, flowers were thrown to marching columns of troops, cheering and weeping crowds thronged the railway stations to bid them farewell. Everybody was singing or humming the latest smash hit, 'Just wait, just wait, Serbia you dog!' But Hungary, thanks in part to the obstinate parsimony of her Diet with regard to defence expenditure, was woefully ill-prepared for war. Belying the dazzling uniforms of its elite regiments, the Dual Monarchy's army was poorly armed and poorly trained. During the first four weeks of hostilities alone Austria-Hungary lost 250,000 men, dead and wounded, while over 100,000 of the Monarchy's troops had been taken prisoner. Of these losses, Hungary's share was over 40 per cent. Few Hungarian families were spared. After six months, the professional army had been virtually wiped out; henceforth the Monarchy would have to rely on conscripts.

In the Hungarian political establishment, very few voices had been raised against Hungary's close alignment with Germany or against the war which – since Austria-Hungary could not have acted without German backing – resulted from it. One of them belonged to Count Mihály Károlyi, who in May 1914 had told a political meeting: *I want a foreign policy in which we have a free hand and are not sycophants of German imperialism … We should draw nearer to France and Russia and thus insure our Balkan interests.*[3] When war broke out, Károlyi was rushing back from a visit to the United States and got as far as France, where he was interned for several weeks in Bordeaux as an enemy alien (although he was an ardent Francophile). Both he and Count István Bethlen, despite their immunity from conscription as Members of Parliament, volunteered to serve as cavalry officers. They were both destined to play leading roles in their country's troubled future.

2
Mihály Károlyi and István Bethlen

Count Mihály Károlyi and Count István Bethlen shared noble birth and, eventually, political ambition. They had little else in common.

Károlyi, like many members of the European aristocracy, was a victim of in-breeding; his parents were first cousins, from two of Hungary's most eminent and wealthiest families – the Károlyi estates were among the two or three largest in the country. Mihály was a sickly child born, in March 1875, with a cleft palate, a hare lip and nearly blind in one eye. He could barely make himself understood until, when he was 14, a risky but successful operation on his palate gave him the possibility of intelligible speech. Daily voice exercises, at which he persisted with remarkable determination, eventually enabled him to speak almost normally. Mihály's mother died of tuberculosis shortly after his birth and his father had no time for a handicapped offspring; he was therefore brought up by an over-protective grandmother. As is often the case, Károlyi's physical handicaps propelled him into a whirlwind of activity designed to show that he could and had overcome

COUNT MIHÁLY KÁROLYI (1875–1955)
'Mihály Károlyi, when I first glimpsed him on the streets of Pest wearing his broad-brimmed, flat, arty hat – you had to be a Count to get away with sporting such a white hat – had still looked very much like the type of young magnate the ordinary Budapest mortal might see at the racetrack or behind the fence of the Park Club. It was not difficult to imagine him sunk into one of the easy chairs at the National Casino where it would never occur to the yawning, infinitely bored lounger to get up and stroll over to the library. One could picture him at the gaming table, losing sums that are phenomenal in the history of Hungarian gambling ... Likewise, we may picture him at golf, tennis or yachting – in any way except in the very position that the mysterious hand of fate was to mete out for him ... But some future author of historical novels who will select, from his cool-headed distant perspective, the extraordinary life of Mihály Károlyi as his subject, will be able to see this fated figure with greater clarity than we who knew him personally. It is said that nothing happens by accident, but an examination of Mihály Károlyi's incalculable career must shatter all our beliefs in notions of purposefulness, calculated careers and conscious planning. Instead, we are reminded of the unknown forces that create tremors deep underground or turbulence in the stratosphere. For it must have been from deep underground or high up in the air that the spirit emerged to guide the affairs of this bearded young man who sauntered by on the Budapest street, this impassive and nonchalant dandy, whose only worry seemed to be deciding what to do on this boring, endless summer day ... The next time I saw him was in the Prime Minister's office ...' (From *Károlyi's Strange Career* (1925) by Gyula Krudy, translated by John Bátki).

them. He played polo, drove fast cars and gambled recklessly with the family fortune in the Casino.

More seriously, he read widely in English and, maintaining his family's Francophone tradition, in French. In his early twenties, he spent several years in Paris and visited both England and the United States. Partly under the influence of his uncle, Sándor Károlyi, who had founded the agricultural co-operative movement in Hungary, Mihály flirted with socialism, read Karl Marx and met Sidney and Beatrice Webb in London. Aged 26, he stood for Parliament as an Independence Party candidate and, because he refused to conform to the normal practice in Hungary of buying votes, lost. He had better luck in 1910, benefiting from his prestige as the newly elected President of the National Hungarian Agricultural Society, and duly took his seat in the Lower Chamber on the opposition benches. The Independence Party endeavoured to keep alive the principles of Lajos Kossuth – full independence for Hungary, less dependence on Germany and social reform; the radical wing of the party, to which Károlyi soon gravitated, also favoured universal suffrage. When, in 1912, István Tisza used strong-arm tactics to secure the passage through Parliament of the controversial Army Bill (which committed Hungary to paying a larger share of the Monarchy's defence expenditure) Károlyi insulted him in terms which resulted in a duel (although technically illegal, duelling was still, in Hungary, the recognised manner of resolving issues of honour between gentlemen); when, after 34 bouts, Károlyi sustained the first cut, the fight was stopped. In 1914, the complications of Károlyi's personal life, which included a long and hopeless affair with a married woman and a mountain of debt incurred at the tables of the Casino, were resolved by a brilliant marriage – to Catherine (Katinka or 'Katus') Andrássy, the attractive, intelligent and independent-minded granddaughter of Count Gyula Andrássy, the Dual Monarchy's exceptionally talented Foreign Minister in the 1870s. As well as belonging to one of Hungary's most distinguished families, Catherine was related to virtually all the others – the Zichys, the Pálffys, the Eszterházys, the Batthyánys and the Odescalchi's to name but a few. Given the trials to which it was to be subjected, the marriage was extraordinarily successful. It was typical of the age – at least in Hungary – that when Károlyi volunteered for military service after the outbreak of war in 1914, he was at once appointed ADC to the commanding officer of his cavalry regiment so that the life of such a prominent landowner and politician should not be put at risk in the front line. An even more telling social commentary lay in the fact that the departure of the regiment for the Galician front, where it was desperately needed, was delayed for several months until Károlyi's young wife had safely delivered their first-born.

Meanwhile, the career of István Bethlen had developed along very similar lines to that of Mihály Károlyi. Born into a prominent landowning family in Transylvania in 1874, young István lost his father at the age of eight and, in effect, his mother as well – Countess Ilona Bethlen, shattered by her husband's premature death, withdrew into the shadows of chronic depression. István, as decreed by his father's will, was packed off to the Theresianum in Vienna, an educational establishment founded by Maria Theresa for the children of the Monarchy's aristocracy and designed to cement their loyalty to the crown; its academic standards were high and its ethos similar to that of an English 19th-century public school. István stayed there until the age of 18 and performed well. In common with the Theresianum's other star pupils, he was appointed a royal page. When he emerged from this rigorously disciplined hothouse, the principles which were to underlie his future political life had largely been formed. Although in many respects a liberal, Bethlen believed passionately in the mission of the nobility to lead the nation and in István Széchenyi's philosophy of gradualism rather than in Kossuth's radicalism. Like Mihály Károlyi, however, he was attracted by Count Sándor Károlyi's co-operative movement and resolved to promote it in his native Transylvania.

As a law student at the University of Budapest – where he and Károlyi may have first met – Bethlen celebrated his escape from the tight reins of the Theresianum by immersing himself in the pleasures of the capital's high society; he managed to graduate, but without distinction. He next spent several months in England, to improve his English and to study British agriculture; he had by now realised that in view of his mother's continuing incapacity it would fall to him to manage the family estates in Transylvania. In further preparation for this task, he spent two years at one of Hungary's leading agricultural institutes before returning to the ancestral home in Transylvania, in one of its less-developed regions with a large Romanian population. He took his duties as a landowner seriously, devoting most of his time and energy to the modernisation of his farms and improvement of their crops and livestock. He travelled widely in Europe and North America but with the principal objective of studying agricultural practice and techniques. He also found time to woo and marry Margit Bethlen – no relation, despite sharing his distinguished Transylvanian name – and to begin a political career. In 1901, standing as a government party candidate, Bethlen was elected to Parliament unopposed.

Bethlen now divided his time between Transylvania and Budapest. Particularly after Margit had given birth to their third son in 1906, their marriage cooled and Bethlen resumed the amorous adventures in Budapest which he had begun as a university student. In Parliament, he concentrated mainly on agricultural issues and on promoting the interests of Sándor Károlyi's Co-operative of Hungarian Farmers, of which he became Vice-President. Like Mihály Károlyi, Bethlen was also active in the National Hungarian Agricultural Society. Bethlen shared Mihály Károlyi's distaste for Prime Minister István Tisza's unscrupulous methods of parliamentary management. Indeed, when in 1912 Tisza's tactics in forcing through the Army Bill from the Speaker's chair provoked brawls in the chamber and police intervention, Bethlen helped to rescue Károlyi from the clutches of the gendarmes: 'clothing was hanging from Károlyi in shreds and he even lost consciousness for a few minutes, for all the support of his friends.'[1] Bethlen had by then deserted Tisza's governing Party of Work, joining the Independence Party – like Károlyi – in 1905. Károlyi had not yet been converted to the cause of universal suffrage; he and Bethlen were both active members of the misleadingly named National Movement for Suffrage Reform, which favoured only a very limited extension of the franchise.

> The segment of the population [i.e. the landowning class] which has always favoured progress because of its cultural superiority, its economic power, its political sophistication, should hold on to this supremacy and hegemony, for the sake of all citizens of this nation, in the future as well.
>
> ISTVÁN BETHLEN, 1910[2]

Bethlen also began actively to support measures to preserve the hegemony of Magyar landowners in Transylvania against encroachment by the Romanian majority and the growing threat of the eventual union of Transylvania with Romania, which had become the primary objective of Romanian foreign policy. On both issues – franchise reform and policy towards the 'nationalities' – Bethlen and Károlyi were soon to part company and to become bitter political opponents.

The Romanian issue, and Bethlen's preoccupation with it, became particularly acute after the outbreak of war in 1914.

Bethlen had been elected two years earlier to the Chairman-ship of the National Hungarian Association, a right-wing body founded to oppose and where possible thwart the aspi-rations of Hungary's ethnic minorities to achieve autonomy or union with their neighbouring motherlands. Romania stepped up her attempts to blackmail the Central Powers (Germany and Austria-Hungary) into granting autonomy to Transylvania, which would inevitably lead to union with Romania, in return for her continued neutrality in the war. Given Romania's strategic importance, Kaiser Wilhelm and Emperor Franz Josef pressed the Hungarians to accept this bargain. Shuttling between his hussar regiment at the front and Parliament in Budapest, Bethlen played a key role in stiff-ening István Tisza's resistance to this pressure. Tisza even-tually persuaded the two Emperors and their ministers that the solution to the problem lay not in giving way to Roma-nian blackmail, but in wooing Bulgaria into alliance with the Central Powers, thus isolating and neutralising Romania. This strategy bought time for Hungary but, as events were soon to show, did not dispose of the problem.

As the nationalities issue and that of franchise reform edged Bethlen towards the right wing of the Independence Party, Hungary's mounting misfortunes in the war and his conversion to the cause of universal suffrage moved Károlyi further to the left and eventually out of the Party altogether. By September 1916, after the Russian General Brusilov's offen-sive had overwhelmed the Monarchy's Fourth and Seventh Armies in Galicia, Austria-Hungary had sustained 750,000 casualties, killed or severely wounded, while 380,000 soldiers had been taken prisoner. Military supplies and medical serv-ices had virtually collapsed; war profiteers made fortunes by supplying the army with paper boots and other sub-standard equipment. At home, food shortages had become acute, the black market flourished and inflation soared. Public enthusiasm for the war evaporated, helped on its way by a succession of compulsory war loans. The reverses suffered by the Central Powers encouraged Romania to abandon her neutrality and to sell her support to the Allies in return for the promise of Transylvania and other slices of Hungarian territory when the war had been won. But Romania was not prepared to wait: as soon as the secret treaty with the Allies had been signed, in August 1916, half a million Romanian troops invaded Transylvania and were soon poised to advance into the Hungarian heartland. Hungary was saved by her German ally; a German army, transferred from the Western Front, counter-attacked in Transylvania, drove the Romanians out in a matter of weeks and occupied most of their country, including Bucharest. Thousands of Transylvania's Romanian population fled their homes and followed the retreating Romanian army across the frontier; many of those who remained were arrested and interned, an operation in which István Bethlen was appointed by the Hungarian government to play a leading role. Bethlen's concerns over Romanian hegemony in Transylvania were allayed – for the time being.

Austro-Hungarian morale soon suffered a further blow. On 21 November 1916, Emperor Franz Josef died at the age of 86. Loyalty to the ageing Emperor, the symbol of the Dual Monarchy's durability and stability, had been an important factor in holding his heterogeneous empire, and especially his polyglot army, together. (It has been calculated that every thousand men in the Monarchy's army was made up of 267 Austrian-Germans, 223 Magyars, 135 Czechs, 85 Poles, 81 Ruthenes, 67 Croats and Serbs, 64 Romanians, 38 Slovaks, 26 Slovenes and 14 Italians.) Franz Josef's 29-year-old successor, his great-nephew Charles (Emperor Karl I of Austria), a weak, impressionable but obstinate young man, was unlikely to command the same degree of devotion. A close associate of the murdered Archduke Franz Ferdinand, Charles was known to share the latter's anti-Magyar views: István Tisza, with his usual political adroitness, ensured his speedy coronation as King Charles IV of Hungary before he had time to tamper with the constitution of the Monarchy to Hungary's disadvantage. Charles's accession was not, however, unwelcome to Mihály Károlyi. In July, Károlyi had led 29 members of Parliament out of the Independence Party to form a new party, the 'Independence & '48 Party', soon known simply as the 'Károlyi Party', whose mission was to oppose the war, to campaign for a separate peace without annexations and to fight for universal suffrage with a secret ballot. These objectives were wholly in line with the views of the new monarch, who on the day after his succession promised to do his utmost 'to put an end to the horrors and sacrifices of the war at the earliest possible moment'.[3] Charles also lost no time in attempting to exert pressure on István Tisza to introduce franchise reform.

Mihály Károlyi showed great moral courage in repeatedly speaking out against the war in Parliament and braving the inevitable charges from the government side of treachery and cowardice. He was, however, sustained by the knowledge that the tide of events had begun to favour his campaign. In March, 1917, the Monarchy's Foreign Minister, Count Czernin, told the German Chancellor: 'The Monarchy is exhausted. Everything possible must be done to draw the necessary conclusions from this sad situation ... Every opportunity must be taken to conclude an acceptable peace.'[4] Czernin also warned his sovereign: 'It is quite obvious that our military strength is coming to an end. Besides, the danger of revolution ... The statesman who is neither blind nor deaf must be aware how the dull despair of the population increases day by day; he is bound to hear the sullen grumbling of the great masses.'[5] Unlike their German ally, whose leaders were confident that the German state would survive even final military defeat, the sovereign and statesmen of the Austro-Hungarian Monarchy realised that if the Central Powers were to lose the war – as seemed increasingly probable – the Monarchy would face disintegration or dismantlement; they were consequently more disposed than the Germans to think in terms of concluding a negotiated peace. When, in January 1917, the Allies included in a public statement of their war aims 'the liberation of the Italians, as also of the Slavs, Roumanians and Czechoslovaks from foreign domination' – in other words, the dismemberment of the Monarchy – it looked as if it was already too late; but the American President Wilson's 'Fourteen Points', set out before the US Senate a week later, spoke less provocatively of national self-determination and, in Article X, demanded that 'the peoples of Austria-Hungary … should be accorded the freest opportunity to autonomous development'.

Mihály Károlyi and his party chose to interpret these formulations as support for complete Hungarian independence from Austria. István Tisza's reaction, in a major speech to Parliament, was more sophisticated: 'The entire Magyar public favours the free development of nations. The principle of national self-determination, however, can be applied fully only where nations live within clearly defined ethnic frontiers. In territories where many peoples and nations live together, it is impossible that all of them should form a national state. There, either a supranational state comes into existence or a state [e.g. Hungary] where the national character is derived from the nation which is the dominant one in the region.'[6]

As the months of 1917 passed, however, the Monarchy's prospects of moving towards an early or separate peace diminished. In an ill-advised initiative, Charles IV used his brother-in-law, Prince Sixtus, who was serving in the Belgian army, as the intermediary for a secret approach to President Poincaré of France in which he undertook to support the French claim to Alsace-Lorraine in any peace settlement. Inevitably, this undertaking was leaked by the French and infuriated the German Kaiser, who exacted retribution by bullying Charles into accepting virtual military and economic union between the German Empire and the Monarchy, thus almost reducing the latter to satellite status and extinguishing the possibility of further peace feelers without German sanction. Moreover, the collapse of the Russian war effort after the February Revolution encouraged many, including Tisza and István Bethlen, to believe that victory for the Central Powers might still be possible. Their armies achieved a massive and unexpected victory over the Italians at Caporetto in October; Romania had been knocked out of the war; and unrestricted submarine warfare appeared to be winning Germany mastery of the high seas. Hungary's internal situation, however, remained dire, particularly after the poor harvest of 1917. Tisza, forced by Charles to resign for his continued opposition to franchise reform, still commanded a majority in Parliament and used it to hold successive weak coalition governments, in one of which Mihály Károlyi held office for the first time, to ransom.

Károlyi now began to adopt a more radical political profile, arguing not only for an end to the German alliance, a complete break with Austria and universal suffrage but also for significant concessions to the 'nationalities'. In October, he held talks with leading representatives of the Slovaks, Romanians, Serbs and Croats and was encouraged by the relative

PRESIDENT WILSON'S FOURTEEN POINTS, 8 JANUARY 1918

The program of the world's peace, therefore, is our program; and that program, the only possible program, as we see it, is this:

I. Open covenants of peace, openly arrived at, after which there shall be no private international understandings of any kind but diplomacy shall proceed always frankly and in the public view.

II. Absolute freedom of navigation upon the seas, outside territorial waters, alike in peace and in war, except as the seas may be closed in whole or in part by international action for the enforcement of international covenants.

III. The removal, so far as possible, of all economic barriers and the establishment of an equality of trade conditions among all the nations consenting to the peace and associating themselves for its maintenance.

IV. Adequate guarantees given and taken that national armaments will be reduced to the lowest point consistent with domestic safety.

V. A free, open-minded, and absolutely impartial adjustment of all colonial claims, based upon a strict observance of the principle that in determining all such questions of sovereignty the interests of the populations concerned must have equal weight with the equitable claims of the government whose title is to be determined.

VI. The evacuation of all Russian territory and such a settlement of all questions affecting Russia as will secure the best and freest cooperation of the other nations of the world in obtaining for her an unhampered and unembarrassed opportunity for the independent determination of her own political development and national policy and assure her of a sincere welcome into the society of free nations under institutions of her own choosing; and, more than a welcome, assistance also of every kind that she may need and may herself desire. The treatment accorded Russia by her sister nations in the months to come will be the acid test of their good will, of their comprehension of her needs as distinguished from their own interests, and of their intelligent and unselfish sympathy.

VII. Belgium, the whole world will agree, must be evacuated and restored, without any attempt to limit the sovereignty which she enjoys in common with all other free nations. No other single act will serve as this will serve to restore confidence among the nations in the laws which they have themselves set and determined for the government of their relations with one another. Without this healing act the whole structure and validity of international law is forever impaired.

VIII. All French territory should be freed and the invaded portions restored, and the wrong done to France by Prussia in 1871 in the matter of Alsace-Lorraine, which has unsettled the peace of the world for nearly fifty years, should be righted, in order that peace may once more be made secure in the interest of all.

IX. A readjustment of the frontiers of Italy should be effected along clearly recognizable lines of nationality.

X. The peoples of Austria-Hungary, whose place among the nations we wish to see safeguarded and assured, should be accorded the freest opportunity to autonomous development.

XI. Rumania, Serbia, and Montenegro should be evacuated; occupied territories restored; Serbia accorded free and secure access to the sea; and the relations of the several Balkan states to one another determined by friendly counsel along historically established lines of allegiance and nationality; and international guarantees of the political and economic independence and territorial integrity of the several Balkan states should be entered into.

XII. The Turkish portion of the present Ottoman Empire should be assured a secure sovereignty, but the other nationalities which are now under Turkish rule should be assured an undoubted security of life and an absolutely unmolested opportunity of autonomous development, and the Dardanelles should be permanently opened as a free passage to the ships and commerce of all nations under international guarantees.

XIII. An independent Polish state should be erected which should include the territories inhabited by indisputably Polish populations, which should be assured a free and secure access to the sea, and whose political and economic independence and territorial integrity should be guaranteed by international covenant.

XIV. A general association of nations must be formed under specific covenants for the purpose of affording mutual guarantees of political independence and territorial integrity to great and small states alike.

moderation of their demands to urge the King to conclude a separate peace while there was still time to settle the 'nationality question' on terms which would protect the integrity of his Hungarian kingdom. The Romanian community even petitioned Archduke Josef, Charles's viceroy in Hungary, to appoint Károlyi to the premiership. Meanwhile, conditions in Hungary during 1918 were going from bad to worse. Yet another bad harvest created a critical shortage of flour while the shortage of coal threatened to bring industry and the railways to a standstill. With the disappearance of an eastern front, Hungary had several hundred thousand more troops than were needed to man the remaining Italian and Balkan fronts; left idle, they began to pose a threat to public order and the country's internal stability. Whole divisions were encamped in railway sidings. Tens of thousands deserted their regiments and headed for home. They were joined on the streets, moreover, by nearly half a million former prisoners of war whom the Bolsheviks had released from camps in Russia. A mutiny in the Austro-Hungarian fleet was followed by another by the army garrison in Pécs, in southern Hungary. The use of military force to suppress a strike in one of Budapest's largest industrial plants precipitated a general strike in the capital. In Parliament, Tisza's relentless use of his majority destroyed successive coalition governments and emasculated their feeble attempts at electoral reform.

By the autumn, Mihály Károlyi and his small party constituted the only genuine and responsible parliamentary opposition and the only group whose objectives – a separate peace with the Allies, universal and secret suffrage and social reform – reflected the aspirations of a weary and desperate Hungarian people.

3
Collapse and Revolution

Once the final Austro-Hungarian offensive on the Italian front, in June 1918, had failed disastrously, with heavy loss of life, the Monarchy fell apart with astonishing speed.

On 16 October 1918 King-Emperor Charles, hoping to give the Monarchy a status more acceptable to an eventual peace conference, signed a manifesto proclaiming Austria to be a federal state 'in which each racial component shall form its own state organisation in its territory of settlement' – but 'maintaining the integrity of the lands that belong to the holy Hungarian Crown'. In other words, Hungary's national minorities were still to be denied the political autonomy which was now being granted to their counterparts in the Austrian Empire; the Hungarian Prime Minister, Wekerle, had secured this qualification to the manifesto only by threatening to suspend deliveries of flour and grain to Austria. On the following day István Tisza, the staunchest advocate of continuing the war until final victory, rose from his seat in Parliament to declare: 'I will not play with words. I must acknowledge the truth of what Mihály Károlyi said in his speech yesterday. We have lost the war.' [1] News of this admission spread through the lands of the Monarchy like wildfire, to devastating effect. The steady trickle of desertions from the army became a flood. On 20 October, the Hungarian Parliament voted to revoke the Compromise of 1867, thus breaking all Hungary's historic ties with Austria except that of sharing a common monarch – for a little longer, Charles IV remained king. Shortly afterwards, on Mihály Károlyi's initiative, the Social Democratic Party and the Radical Citizens' Party joined the Károlyi Party in forming a National Council under Károlyi's chairmanship; its first manifesto called for full independence for Hungary, an immediate end to the war and to the German alliance, universal suffrage, land reform and self-determination for the 'nationalities'. Hungary now had an alternative government. It was already clear, however, that when it came to power it would govern a different and smaller nation: the 'nationalities' were taking matters into their own hands. In Bukovina, a Romanian National Council declared its secession from the Monarchy; in Prague, the Czechs and Slovaks proclaimed a Czechslovak Republic; and in Zagreb the Croatian parliament announced the creation of the independent state of Croatia-Slavonia within the new federation of South Slavs, the future Yugoslavia. Within the space of just a few days, the Dual Monarchy had fallen apart.

On 31 October, two events marked the end of the old political order. In the afternoon, a group of deserters broke into István Tisza's private villa in Pest and after a short altercation in the hallway about responsibility for the war, shot Tisza dead in front of his wife and niece. His butler had warned him that his life was in danger and had advised Tisza to escape by jumping out of a rear window. Tisza had refused to flee: 'I shall not jump anywhere. I wish to die upright, the way I have lived.' [2] At about the same time, Archduke Josef, acting on behalf of the king, appointed Count Mihály Károlyi Prime Minister.

Even before his formal appointment to head the government, Károlyi had become the acknowledged leader of his country. Sándor Wekerle and his cabinet had resigned, leaving Hungary without a government. Károlyi had called on Charles IV at the King's country palace outside Budapest and came away under the impression that Charles had accepted the National Council's programme and had asked him to head a new government; he travelled by train to Vienna, where the oath of office would be administered. In fact, Charles had already appointed a more conservative figure, Count János Hadik, to the premiership and Károlyi's journey was fruitless. He returned to Budapest to find its populace enraged both by Hadik's appointment and by Charles's despatch of Archduke Josef to exercise royal authority in Hungary – Hungary was still a monarchy and the King, or his viceroy, retained the right to appoint a Prime Minister. Huge crowds were awaiting the arrival of Károlyi's train, singing the 'Marseillaise'; when he jumped into a cab to escape the crush, they unharnessed the horses and pulled it themselves. Soldiers and students were demonstrating in front of the Károlyi mansion on University Square, calling for a republic; and large crowds filled the streets around the Hotel Astoria, where the National Council had established its headquarters. Officers and soldiers flocked there to pledge their allegiance to the Council.

White flowers, asters, on sale everywhere in preparation for All Souls' Day, became the badge of what had now become a revolution: soldiers pinned them to their caps, civilians wore them in their button-holes. Károlyi recorded in his diary: *Lorries, laden with singing, cheering, yelling soldiers and covered with white chrysanthemums, thundered past – rashly driven vehicles are one of the symptoms of revolution.*[3] The revolution soon had its first martyrs. When a large crowd attempted to cross the Chain Bridge in order to storm Archduke Josef's palace on the Buda side, police blocked its way and opened fire: three people were killed and some 70 injured. Archduke Josef still had at his disposal the Budapest military garrison, which the National Council now determined to subvert, sending emissaries to the barracks to encourage the formation of Soldiers' Councils, following the example of the Russian army in February 1917. Supporters of the National Council occupied the main public buildings in Pest, including the railway stations and telephone exchanges. Prisoners were released from the city's gaols. Imperial crests and insignia were torn down. Hadik resigned the premiership to make way for Károlyi. On 13 November, Charles IV bowed to the inevitable and abdicated the Hungarian crown; three days later, the Hungarian Parliament dissolved itself and, beneath the great dome of the Parliament Building, the Hungarian Republic was proclaimed.

In turning to Károlyi, in many ways an unlikely leader, the Hungarian public voiced its belief that his opposition to the war and open sympathy for the Allies would enable him to conclude peace more quickly and, above all, on more favourable terms than any other Hungarian politician could hope to secure. Károlyi had quickly attempted to meet these expectations. On the Italian front, an armistice had already been negotiated by the local military commanders; it provided for the withdrawal of Austro-Hungarian troops from South Tyrol, Croatia, Istria and Dalmatia – regions in which Italy had long aspired to establish a presence. On the southern, Balkan front no armistice had yet been agreed. Károlyi therefore hastened to Belgrade, with a delegation which included the new Minister for National Minorities, Oszkár Jászi, to negotiate with the French commander of the Allied armies in the Balkans, General Franchet d'Esperey, and thus to forestall any further advance of Allied troops into Hungarian territory. The opening exchanges were not promising. Károlyi read out a memorandum, agreed by his cabinet, which disclaimed responsibility for the actions of Hungary's former leaders, stressed the new government's commitment to democracy and requested that, if Hungary had to be occupied, it should be by Allied troops and not by Czechs, Romanians or Serbs.

If Károlyi had hoped that this declaration of virtue and good intent would soften French hearts, he was disappointed. Franchet d'Esperey responded by giving the Hungarians a brutal dressing-down: Hungary had been an accomplice of Germany since 1867 and would have to suffer with her. The Magyars had suppressed Hungary's national minorities: 'The Czechs, Slovaks, Romanians and Yugoslavs are your enemies. I have only to give a signal and you will be destroyed.'[4] He even made disparaging remarks about the inclusion of a Jew and a common soldier (representing the new Soldiers' Council) in the Hungarian delegation. Once he had got the bile out of his system, however,

THE BÁNÁT
The Bánát was a region of southern Hungary bordering on Serbia, with a mixed population of ethnic Germans, Magyars, Romanians and Serbs, long coveted by both Romania and Serbia; it roughly corresponded to the Vojvodina in former Yugoslavia together with the south-western corner of Romania.

the General proved to be a reasonable negotiator. Taking Károlyi and Jászi into a private room, he handed them the text of the armistice terms which had been drawn up in Paris to apply to the Central Powers and their allies. The terms were harsh. Hungary was to withdraw her troops from the eastern two-thirds of Transylvania and from a large area of the south of the country, including the Bánát which would be occupied by Serbian troops.

The Hungarian army was to be limited to eight divisions; and Allied forces were to have the right of free passage through all Hungarian territory. Clause 17 of the document stated that, pending the signature of a peace treaty, the Hungarian government would retain the right to administer all of Hungary, including those areas occupied by Allied troops; but that in the event of disorder, the Allies would take over the functions of government. Károlyi argued that this qualification would simply encourage the 'nationalities' to foment disorder, if economic hardship had not caused them already. Franchet d'Esperey agreed to omit the offending clause – a significant concession – and to telegraph to Paris the Hungarian delegation's request that until a peace treaty had been concluded the Allies should respect Hungary's existing frontiers and protect the country against attacks by Czechs, Romanians or Serbs. This plea merely evoked from Clemenceau, the French Prime Minister, a brusque injunction to General Franchet d'Esperey to confine his discussions exclusively to military matters. When Károlyi, on his return to Budapest, laid the armistice terms before the National Council the decision was taken to accept them, if only to set some limit to the incursions by Czech and Romanian troops which were already taking place; their publication in the Hungarian press nevertheless caused a wave of public bitterness and disappointment which marked the beginning of a general loss of confidence in Károlyi and his regime.

Hungary's situation now became more desperate with every day that passed. In the north-west, Czech troops had advanced into Hungary as far as Pozsony (Bratislava), former seat of the Hungarian Parliament; with difficulty, Hungarian troops loyal to Károlyi drove them back. The Czechs had already cut off Hungary's main source of coal, the mines of Slovakia, causing widespread hardship in a harsh winter. Romania, despite having concluded a separate peace with the Central Powers in the Treaty of Bucharest, following her defeat by the Germans in 1916, had re-entered the war on the side of the Allies in November in order to claim a share of the spoils; and now demanded recognition of her annexation of the whole of Transylvania. Károlyi made repeated appeals to the Allied leaders, who were beginning to assemble in Paris in preparation for the Peace Conference, for their intervention to stop these flagrant violations of the Belgrade armistice and to compel the Czechs to lift their economic blockade. His appeals were ignored. The French, recognised by her allies as having the leading role in East-Central Europe and the Balkans, argued successfully that Hungary, a defeated enemy, had no claim to favourable treatment; the interests of the Czechs, Romanians and South Slavs, fellow Allies, should be given priority.

The month of November was marked by two arrivals in Budapest which were to have ominous implications for Hungary's immediate future. First, on the 24th, a group of Hungarians arrived from Moscow, former prisoners of war in Russia who had been converted to communism during their captivity: Béla Kun, Tibor Szamuely, Ferenc Münnich and Mátyás Rákosi at once set about founding the Hungarian Communist Party. Two days later, a French Military Mission arrived to supervise the implementation of the Belgrade Armistice Agreement; it was led by a Lieutenant-Colonel Fernand Vyx. Vyx's first task was to transmit to Károlyi the Allies' demand that Hungarian troops should withdraw from the Slovak territory which, in contravention of the terms of the armistice, had been invaded by the Czechs. Clinging to the hope that the eventual peace treaty would put all wrongs to rights, Károlyi complied; the Czechs forthwith occupied the historic Hungarian towns of Kassa (Košice) and Pozsony. Meanwhile, Serbian troops had pushed northwards to occupy the area near Pécs which contained Hungary's last remaining coal mines; and the Romanians advanced further into Transylvania. The Belgrade Armistice was already a dead letter.

> My foreign policy is based on Wilsonian ideals. We have only one ideology: Wilson, Wilson and for the third time Wilson.
>
> MIHÁLY KÁROLYI,
> 30 DECEMBER 1918[5]

Károlyi was powerless to prevent, much less reverse, these setbacks. He continued to pin his faith on the Peace Conference, which was shortly to open in Paris, and in particular on President Wilson and his Fourteen Points which, he believed, could act as midwife for the birth of a new Hungary, perhaps restructured on the lines of the Swiss Confederation.

In the meantime, he had other issues to address. His coalition government had begun to break up on the proposed legislation for land reform, which was too radical for the right wing of his party and not radical enough for the Social Democrats. To resolve this crisis, Károlyi resigned the premiership on 11 January 1919 and assumed the office of President of the Republic – the young Republic had hitherto lacked a head of state – while retaining responsibility for foreign policy. A new cabinet was formed, under Dénes Berinkey as Prime Minister, with a more leftist complexion than its predecessor. This fuelled the attempts of Hungarian conservatives, and in particular of István Bethlen who opposed every aspect of the Károlyi regime's policies, to undermine Károlyi's authority by warning the French Mission and other Allied representatives that Károlyi represented the first stage of Hungary's drift into Bolshevism. The French were only too ready to believe this. Indeed, Károlyi himself had begun to fear that if the Big Three (France, Great Britain and the United States) did not heed Hungary's pleas for an end to the economic blockade against her – a hangover from the war which had not been removed when hostilities ceased – and to the invasion of her territory by her neighbours, the Hungarian people might well turn to Communism, and to the newly established Hungarian Communist Party, in desperation.

Meanwhile, the Peace Conference had opened in Paris on 18 January, presided over by the Supreme Council. The Council, which before the cessation of hostilities had been the Supreme War Council, consisted of the leaders of the United States, Great Britain, France, Italy and Japan, with their Foreign Ministers. Once the Peace Conference was under way, the Council became known as the Council of Ten; later, in March 1919, this shrank to become the Council of Four – President Woodrow Wilson and Prime Ministers David Lloyd George, Georges Clemenceau and Vittorio Orlando. Soon after the opening of the Conference, the Council despatched an Allied mission to Budapest to assess Hungary's economic situation. At the mission's first meeting with the Hungarian President, Károlyi did not mince his words. The Hungarian people had given him power, he told them, in the belief that he could communicate with the Allies; he had been unable to do so because the Allies refused to listen. Hungary had not been invited to send representatives to the Peace Conference in Paris: it was wholly unjust that her future frontiers should be determined in her absence. Hungary's economic situation was disastrous: the peasants could not gather in the potato harvest for lack of boots and coats; mainline trains had been reduced to one a day for lack of coal; there were no dairy products in the shops. The Allied delegates were unmoved. The French representative simply retorted that the situation in Belgium and Northern France was far worse. There could be no negotiation with 'enemy states' before the conclusion of a peace treaty. Other members of the mission took Károlyi to task for failing to arrest the leaders of Hungary's Communist Party. The British delegate, William Beveridge, recorded in his diary: 'I found myself explaining to him [Mihály Károlyi] ... that I did not think that the Entente had any particular dislike for Hungary, or any deliberate intention to harm, in leaving them so long unnoticed; the Entente Governments had many more important things to think about than the fate of 10,000,000 people in Hungary, and Hungary must wait her turn for political attention.'[6]

On returning to Paris, Beveridge nevertheless argued in his report that the embargo on trade with Hungary should be lifted and diplomatic relations established with the Károlyi regime. A second, American-led, Allied mission, despatched from Paris to assess the political situation in Hungary, also reported sympathetically. The Supreme Council ignored both reports. In February 1919, a British Military Mission, led by Colonel Thomas Cunninghame, arrived in Budapest to work alongside the French. Cunninghame, a man of decidedly right-wing views, regarded Károlyi and the new Hungarian cabinet with some suspicion and reacted with hostility to repeated warnings from Hungarian ministers that the Communists would take over unless the Allies intervened; if that were to happen, he replied, the Allies would support a general invasion of Hungary by her hostile neighbours to crush a Communist regime. Cunninghame's reports to his superiors in Paris nevertheless showed sympathetic understanding of

Károlyi's predicament and blamed the Czechs for it. Despite these repeated warnings of the likely consequences of inaction, the Supreme Council obstinately refused to do anything to ameliorate Hungary's disastrous situation.

Under its new Prime Minister, Berinkey, the Hungarian cabinet had finally agreed on a policy for land reform and the redistribution of land from the large estates to the landless peasantry. Károlyi, one of Hungary's largest landowners, insisted on inaugurating the redistribution himself, on his vast estate near Kápolna in north-eastern Hungary. The land reform issue drove Károlyi and Bethlen even further apart.

> The rain was falling heavily on that day in March when I distributed my lands. Peasants from all the different parts of my estate stood under their large umbrellas, their deeply furrowed faces lifted up to me in indescribable amazement, wonder and suspicion.
> MIHÁLY KÁROLYI[7]

One of Hungary's greatest modern writers, the journalist Gyula Krudy, was there: 'In the middle of a broad field there is a platform built of wood, surrounded by several thousand people who have been standing there since morning ... Mihály Károlyi stands on the platform, his uplifted arms point out the fields in the four directions of the compass: *All this was mine until now. From this day on, it belongs to you*! A finer speech was never heard in these parts ...'[8]

This dramatic and symbolic act deserves a mention in any account of Mihály Károlyi's career. It remained, however, an almost unique instance of the implementation of a land reform which elsewhere in Hungary was obstructed by defiant landlords, including István Bethlen in Transylvania, or swept aside by impatient peasants who arbitrarily occupied land regardless of whether it fell within the terms of the reforming legislation. Bethlen was equally strongly opposed to the new electoral law introduced by the Károlyi regime which extended the franchise to most literate men over 21 and to women over 24 – about half the adult population – with a secret ballot. This important measure, however, was also still-born since Hungary's internal situation remained too volatile to allow elections to be called without risking civil war. In February, Bethlen formed an openly counter-revolutionary party, the Party of National Unity, to co-ordinate opposition to Károlyi's presidency and government; he established close links with both Colonel Cunninghame of the British Mission and with Lieutenant-Colonel Vyx of the French. His appeals, through them, for the occupation of Budapest and other cities by Allied troops in order to pre-empt the Communist threat and install a right-wing government were ignored as completely by the Supreme Council as were Károlyi's. They were drowned out by louder and more insistent voices hostile to Hungary.

4

Prelude to Paris

The formal opening of the Paris Peace Conference took place in the Salle d'Horloge in the Quai d'Orsay on 18 January 1919. In a sense, it had been in progress since the outbreak of war nearly five years earlier. Both the Central Powers and the Allies, each assuming that final victory would be theirs, had been planning throughout that period, both publicly and in secret, for the post-war re-arrangement of Europe.

The ambitions and objectives of the German Empire found expression in Friedrich Naumann's treatise on *Mitteleuropa*, published in 1915. This envisaged the permanent union of Germany with Austria-Hungary to create a mega-state, stretching from the Baltic to the Adriatic, which would enjoy unchallenged hegemony over Europe. Enthusiasm in Vienna and Budapest for this project was, to say the least, muted: it was clear that the role envisaged for Austria-Hungary would be that of junior partner. István Tisza instructed Hungarian representatives at official talks about the scheme to take a very cautious line. Tisza's own war aims were confined to the annexation to Hungary of Bosnia-Hercegovina and Dalmatia, to balance Austria's planned acquisition of Russia's share of Poland. He was opposed to the Monarchy's annexation of Serbia, on the grounds that this would simply exacerbate Hungary's 'nationality' problems by substantially increasing the Slav element in her population.

The Allies' objectives were less acquisitive but more complex. On some points there was general agreement. Germany must be deprived of the capability ever again to wage war on her neighbours; Poland, divided for so long between Russia and Austria, must once again become a unitary, independent state; Croatia must be free to determine her own destiny. The future of the Dual Monarchy as such, however, remained a controversial issue almost until the war came to an end. Until 1918, the traditional view that Austria-Hungary constituted an essential component of a European balance of power tended to prevail in ruling circles. Most Allied statesmen viewed the Monarchy as an important barrier against both Russian expansion westwards and, equally, against a renewed German *Drang nach Osten*. When President Wilson addressed the US Congress in December, 1917, on the United States' entry into the war he declared that 'we do not wish in any way to impair or re-arrange the Austro-Hungarian Empire'.[1] When, at about the same time, secret talks took place in Geneva between General Smuts, representing the Allies, and Count Mensdorff of Austria about the possibility of a separate peace for the Monarchy, Smuts assured the Count that: 'We had no intention of interfering in her [Austria-Hungary's] internal affairs but we recognised that if Austria could become a really liberal Empire … she would become for Central Europe very much what the British Empire had become for the rest of the world.'[2]

In other words, the structure and extent of the Monarchy could remain unchanged if its policies towards its national minorities were to be liberalised. And at the beginning of 1918 the British War Cabinet endorsed the view of the Prime Minister, David Lloyd George, that after the war 'Austria-Hungary should be in a position to exercise a powerful influence in south-east Europe'.[3]

These reassuring professions owed a great deal to Allied hopes, especially in 1917, that the Monarchy might be persuaded to desert the Kaiser and conclude a separate peace with the Allies: the Monarchy would obviously be less inclined to enter into such an arrangement if it were given reason to believe that it would be signing up to its own dismemberment. But they were also the essence of hypocrisy, since the Allies had already given away, at least on paper, large chunks of Austro-Hungarian territory as bribes to potential allies. In the secret Treaty of London (1915), Italy had been seduced from neutrality with the promise of Trentino, South Tyrol, Trieste, Gorizia, Istria, northern Dalmatia and most of the Dalmatian islands – all territories which belonged to the Monarchy. Even more at variance with Allied denials of any intent to damage the integrity of the Monarchy were the promises made to Romania in 1916 in return for her entry into the war: Romania was to be rewarded with the whole of Transylvania, the Bánát – both components of historic Hungary – and the Bukovina. Serbia's government-in-exile was promised Bosnia-Hercegovina, recently annexed by the Monarchy, together with south Dalmatia. If, therefore, the Allies did indeed wish the Dual Monarchy to survive as a political expression, it would be an entity significantly reduced in size when these promissory notes were redeemed.

The Allies' professed intentions had, however, increasingly been called into question as the war ground on, both by exiled leaders of the national groupings within the Monarchy who saw in the war their best hope of securing recognition and national independence; and by their active sympathisers within the political establishments of the Allied nations. As early as the autumn of 1914, two seasoned campaigners for Croatian independence from Hungary, Frano Supilo and Dr Ante Trumbić, began to lobby in London for the creation, after the war, of a South Slav (Yugoslav) federation. In April, 1915, a Yugoslav Committee was established in London, under the chairmanship of Dr Trumbić, to promote the creation of a single Yugoslav state which would unite the Serbian, Croatian and Slovene peoples in a federation of equals. The project took a further step forward in 1917 when Nikola Pašić, leader of the Serbian government-in-exile, proposed to the Yugoslav Committee that they should hold a joint conference in Corfu to agree common political aims. The Corfu Conference, held in June, 1917, was a success; agreement was reached on the establishment, post-war, of a Kingdom of Serbs, Croats and Slovenes under the royal Serbian Karadjordjević dynasty. If this agreement were to be endorsed by the Peace Conference, therefore, Hungary would be deprived of Croatia – her oldest possession outside the Magyar heartland – and in all probability of a slice of territory on her southern border in which there was a significant Serb population.

Of even greater importance for Hungary's future were the activities of the champions of an independent state of Czechs and Slovaks. Tomáš Masaryk, a Czech professor of philosophy and a future leader of his people, was hard at work within a month of the outbreak of war lobbying in Paris and London for an independent Bohemia, still a major component of the Austrian Empire within the Austro-Hungarian Monarchy, which would incorporate the predominantly Slovak regions of northern Hungary. In 1916 Masaryk, having formed the

Czechoslovak National Council in Paris and arguing that, far from constituting a barrier to Germany's eastward expansion the Austro-Hungarian Monarchy had become its willing agent, persuaded the French Prime Minister, Aristide Briand, that the Monarchy should be dismembered, and won his support for the creation of an independent Czechoslovak state. Masaryk, who was assisted in his efforts by Eduard Beneš, a bitter enemy of the Habsburgs and all their works, even proposed to the British Foreign Office that the new state should be linked to the future Yugoslavia by a territorial corridor, to be carved out of western Hungary; but the Allies considered this plan to be too radical, at least for the time being.

The champions of independence for their peoples were actively assisted by two British experts on central Europe, Wickham Steed and Robert Seton-Watson. The two men had met several years before the war in Vienna, where Steed was serving as correspondent for the London *Times* and Seton-Watson, a young Scot of independent means and a brilliant linguist, was engaged in research into the history of Austria-Hungary. During the course of his studies Seton-Watson had developed a profound antipathy to the Hungarians and became the self-appointed champion of those peoples whom he perceived as victims of Magyar discrimination and oppression. Steed, who subsequently became Foreign Editor and then Editor of *The Times*, fully shared Seton-Watson's views and used his considerable influence to promote them. In 1916 Seton-Watson founded a journal, *The New Europe*, whose contributors used its pages to argue for the replacement of the Austro-Hungarian Monarchy by a conglomeration of independent nations. British or French experts on east-central Europe and the Balkans were at that time very thin on the ground; the small group of officials, journalists and academics with knowledge and direct experience of the region consequently commanded a degree of influence disproportionate to its size and enjoyed ready access to policy-makers at the highest level, from the Prime Minister downwards. Given the strength of Seton-Watson's views and his passionate commitment to the creation of independent Czechoslovak and Yugoslav states, this was a misfortune for Hungary.

The occasional intemperance of his judgements and the virulence of his Magyar-phobia did not diminish Seton-Watson's impact on the development of Allied planning for post-war Europe, as a British Foreign Office memorandum of 1916 showed. This argued that 'the principle of nationality should ... be one of the governing factors in the consideration of territorial arrangements after the war'. It went on: 'If the situation should be one which enables the Allies to dispose of its future, there seems very little doubt that, in accordance with the principle of giving free play to nationalities, the Dual Monarchy ... should be broken up, as there is no doubt that all the non-German parts of Austria-Hungary will secede.'[5]

'What Prussian militarism is for us, Magyar hegemony is for you [Romanians]: these are the principal obstacles to European progress ... you with the Serbs must put an end to the brutal and artificial domination of the Magyar race over all its neighbours.'

R W SETON-WATSON, INTERVIEWED IN BUCHAREST IN 1915[4]

Across the Atlantic, American thinking was moving in the same direction by 1918. Secretary of State Robert Lansing suggested in a memorandum to President Wilson that the United States should consider whether she should 'favour the disintegration of the Austro-Hungarian empire into its component parts ... giving recognition to the nationalities that seek independence'.[6] Support for this view gathered momentum throughout the Alliance. In June, the Supreme War Council proclaimed its sympathy for the national aspirations of the Czechs, Slovaks and Yugoslavs; and shortly afterwards the United States, in an unequivocal statement which doubtless owed much to the influence of Masaryk who was on a speaking tour of North America, declared that 'all branches of the Slav race should be completely freed from German and Magyar rule'.[7] France, Britain and the United States now recognised Masaryk's Czechoslovak National Council as the trustee of a future Czechoslovak government; on 28 October 1918, the Council proclaimed from Prague the foundation of the Czechoslovak Republic. On the following day, the Croatian parliament in Zagreb declared Croatia to be independent and a future member of a Yugoslav federation. A month later, the Serbian National Council announced the incorporation into Serbia of the southern counties of Hungary (the western Bánát), occupied by Serbian troops. And on 1 December 1918, the Romanian National Assembly, meeting in Gyulafehérvár, Transylvania, proclaimed the union of Transylvania with the Kingdom of Romania.

When, therefore, the Paris Peace Conference opened in January 1919, and before the drafting of peace treaties had even begun, most of its outcome so far as Hungary was concerned had been predetermined. Thanks in large part to the proselytising activities of Masaryk, Beneš, Trumbić, Pašić and others, and to their sympathisers, the Allies were now firmly committed to the independence of the future 'successor states'. Hungary therefore faced the certain loss of Slovakia and Croatia; the probable loss of her southern counties with a predominantly Serb population; and the possible loss of

Admiral Miklós Horthy, mounted on a white horse, leads the National Army into Budapest, 16 November 1919.

II

The Paris Peace Conference

5
Károlyi Abdicates

By the middle of March 1919, the Károlyi government's writ had ceased to run in much of Hungary. In the absence of elections, it lacked a popular mandate; its dogged faith in President Wilson had resulted in nothing but disaster; its land reform had been unveiled too late and was, for many, too little. Hungary had been invaded from the north, east and south by her traditional enemies. Epidemics of typhus and Spanish flu were cutting swathes through a population weakened by hunger and lack of fuel. Károlyi's shortcomings as a national leader were being ruthlessly exposed by events: effective in parliamentary debate among his peers, he lacked the charisma needed by a popular leader to hold a nation together in time of crisis. In the situation in which Hungary now found herself, the high principles and good intentions of a government of well-meaning aristocrats were not enough.

The Social Democrats now commanded wide support throughout the country, although they were unable to prevent or control the wave of strikes by factory workers, printers, waiters, musicians and cab-drivers which afflicted the capital. Moreover, their influence was already being challenged by

BÉLA KUN (1885–1939)
Born into a non-practising Jewish family in Transylvania, Kun was an unpromising student and survived for only one semester in Kolozsvár (Cluj) University's law school. Before the outbreak of war, he combined a career in the local Workers' Insurance Bureau with radical journalism, making a reputation for himself as the scourge of corruption and inefficiency in municipal government. Having enlisted in the army in 1914, Kun was taken prisoner after two years' service on the Russian front and sent to a prisoner-of-war camp in Tomsk, where he formed a Marxist discussion group and contributed articles to *Pravda*. Freed from the camp after Russia's February Revolution, he inserted himself into Lenin's entourage and became leader of the Hungarian Section of the Bolshevik Party. The example of Lenin's pragmatism and tactical skills did not, however, rub off on Kun; he retained the breathless impatience and restless ambition of his youth, drawing up an absurdly simplistic blueprint for European revolution. The 133 days of Communist rule in Hungary demonstrated Kun's lack of long-term vision and his impatience for immediate results; he seemed determined to outdo his mentor and hero, Lenin. After the collapse of his regime and flight to Vienna, Kun reached Russia and joined the Red Army to fight for the Bolsheviks in the Civil War. As chairman of the Crimea Soviet, he achieved notoriety by ordering the execution of nearly 10,000 captured White officers and men; the massacre was condemned even by Trotsky and Stalin. During the 1920s, Kun held a variety of posts in the Comintern, several of them involving clandestine subversive activities in Western Europe. In the 1930s he fell out of favour and in June 1937, was denounced for having a disrespectful attitude to Stalin. He was executed in the Lubyanka on 30 November 1939, aged 53.

the four-month old Communist Party led by Béla Kun. A visiting British journalist, Ellis Ashmead-Bartlett, described Kun in unflattering terms: '[Kun] is a very ugly, bald-headed man, 30 years of age in 1919, of medium height and strongly built. His head is mis-shaped, and his nose and mouth seem to have side-slipped.' [1] Ashmead-Bartlett was not alone: to Stephen Bonsal, an American officer, Kun was a man with 'a

Despite his problems with the Hungarian Communists, Mihály Károlyi was beginning to wonder whether a rapprochement with Moscow might not serve Hungary's interests better than continuing to press her case with the Allies, who remained deaf to his pleas. Faith in President Wilson and his Fourteen Points had brought Hungary nothing. On the other hand, a victorious Red Army was marching into Galicia; and the public mood was swinging decisively to the left. Károlyi's readiness to contemplate a re-orientation of his foreign policy was increased by rumours which were beginning to appear in the Hungarian press of decisions being taken in Paris which would compound Hungary's misfortunes. The rumours were, in fact, well founded. French policy at this time was dominated by the determination of, in particular, Clemenceau and Marshal Foch to strangle Russian Bolshevism before it could infect Europe. The deployment of Allied troops through Romanian territory constituted an essential element of their plans for military intervention in the Ukraine. The French were therefore receptive to Romanian claims, which lacked any foundation, that Hungary was planning an alliance with the Russians against Romania; and to arguments that Romanian troops should be allowed to advance even further into Hungary and should be protected against Hungarian retaliation by the creation of a buffer zone policed by Allied troops. For different reasons – principally the fears expressed by General Franchet d'Esperey concerning the mounting danger of clashes between Hungarian and Romanian troops in eastern Hungary – the Council of Ten had been thinking along similar lines. On 26 February 1919, the Council approved a plan to avert further hostilities by establishing a neutral zone to separate the potential combatants and instructed General Franchet to implement it forthwith.

Lieutenant-Colonel Vyx, head of the French Military Mission in Budapest, had already been displaying a tendency to behave as if he were the Allies' viceroy in Hungary, all but provoking the resignation of the Minister of War, Vilmos Böhm, by his interference in Hungarian military deployments. In the absence of more senior French officers, it fell to Vyx to carry out the Council's instructions. Accompanied by representatives of the other Allied Missions, Vyx called on Mihály Károlyi in the presidential office at 10 a.m. on 20 March and presented him with a formal Note embodying the Council's decision. The Note was, in effect, an ultimatum: the Hungarians were enjoined to respond within 24 hours (the Council had stipulated 48 hours but Vyx apparently reduced this on his own initiative). It significantly enlarged the area of Hungarian territory which Romanian troops were authorised by the Peace Conference to occupy, in effect handing to Romania not only the whole of Transylvania but also a substantial slice of territory to the west of the Transylvanian border; a further area of eastern Hungary was to be designated a neutral zone, occupied by Allied troops.

After reading half the Note, Károlyi sent for Böhm; Vyx suggested that the Prime Minister, Dénes Berinkey, should also join the meeting – a suggestion which Károlyi interpreted as meaning that the Note had political as well as military implications. The question of whether or not the Note was intended to indicate Hungary's future political frontiers has never been satisfactorily resolved. Károlyi and Vilmos Böhm always maintained that Vyx had stated in terms that the new demarcation line should be regarded as the future frontier between Hungary and Romania; according to other accounts, Vyx had been at pains to assert that the Note had purely military significance and that its provisions were designed solely to avert clashes between Hungarian and Romanian forces. Whatever the truth of the matter, Károlyi was clearly justified (as subsequent events proved) in putting the worst interpretation on the contents of the Note and in telling Vyx that it was unacceptable, foreshadowing as it did the future dismemberment of Hungary. Böhm commented that the Note would win 200,000 new members for the Hungarian Communist Party. When Károlyi asked Vyx what would happen if his government decided to reject the Note, Vyx simply replied: 'Alors, nous ferons nos malles' ('We'll pack our bags'), implying that the armistice would be aborted and hostilities against Hungary resumed.

Károlyi immediately summoned an emergency meeting of the cabinet and informed it of the Vyx bombshell. Károlyi proposed that since the Allies themselves had abandoned the Wilsonian principles on which the government had pinned its faith, the coalition should resign and make way for a wholly Social Democratic administration which could unite the country in self-defence and which would be invulnerable, as fellow socialists, to attack by the Russian Soviets; he himself would carry on as President. After some argument, this proposal was accepted; the National Council would dissolve itself and the planned elections further postponed.

A stronger and more determined leader than Mihály Károlyi might have defied the Allied ultimatum and either obliged the Council of Ten to moderate its terms or, if the Council remained adamant, resigned the Presidency in protest; in other words, he could have responded to the Note with an ultimatum of his own. He had some strong cards in his hand. The land reform had restored his popularity in a large section of the Hungarian people; and, as Kun was to show, Hungarians would always respond to a call to arms against Czechs, Romanians and Serbs. It was not, however, in Károlyi's nature to be bold. With the best of motives, he preferred to abdicate to others the responsibility for Hungary's bleak future.

What Károlyi did not know was that the Social Democrats, to whom he intended to transfer power, had already sold out to the Communists. A member of the Social Democratic Central Committee, Jenő Landler, had visited Béla Kun in prison and taken it upon himself to negotiate a merger of the two parties, subject to the Committee's approval. Listening to Landler's report on 21 March, the Committee was undoubtedly influenced by news that 30,000 metalworkers on Csepel island ('Red Csepel') had voted to join the Communist Party *en masse*; and that bands of armed Communist supporters were roaming the streets of the capital. During the afternoon, a deputation of five leading Social Democrats held a brief meeting with Kun in his prison cell, agreed to form a joint Socialist Party of Hungary, accepted the Communist programme *in toto*, promised the Communists ministerial posts in a new cabinet and undertook to work towards an alliance with Bolshevik Russia. When the existing cabinet met at 5 p.m. in order to tender its collective resignation to Károlyi, the Social Democrats did not reveal their arrangements with the Communists, probably because these included Károlyi's removal from the Presidency, merely proposing that the prisoners should be released; this was agreed. In accordance with the cabinet's earlier remit, therefore, Károlyi informed Lieutenant-Colonel Vyx that the cabinet had resigned rather than accept the Allies' ultimatum.

Later, working on his papers in the presidential office, Károlyi was interrupted by his secretary, Henrik Simonyi, who rushed into the room and placed before him a document for his signature: it was a statement that he had resigned the Presidency. When Károlyi refused to sign it, Simonyi told him that the text, over Károlyi's signature, was already being printed in the following morning's newspapers, which would also announce the creation of a dictatorship of the proletariat. To this day, it is unclear whether Károlyi did then sign the document or not; it has never been found. In his memoirs, he denies having done so; others claim that he did sign, reluctantly, accepting an evident *fait accompli*. Whatever the truth, the fact was that Károlyi had been evicted from the Presidency; and that no voice was raised in his defence. By 8 o'clock that evening, all the Communist prisoners had been released. At 10 p.m., the leaders of the new merged Party met to form a Revolutionary Governing Council, under the Chairmanship of a Social Democrat, Sándor Garbai; Kun claimed the post of Commissar for Foreign Affairs. Within the space of a few hours, Hungary had exchanged a liberal-socialist for a Communist regime, a development for which the peacemakers in Paris were largely responsible.

Although he had installed a Social Democrat figurehead as the formal head of the new regime, Béla Kun was from the outset its dominant personality. With extraordinary energy, he set about constructing the whole apparatus of a Communist state. The first proclamation of the Revolutionary Council, issued on 22 March and addressed in Russian Leninist style 'To All, To All!', declared that the Vyx ultimatum would have strangled Hungary; that a dictatorship of the proletariat was necessary to save the Hungarian revolution; that resistance to the new regime would be punishable by death; that a 'gigantic proletarian army' would be created to fight against capitalists, Romanian boyars and Czech bourgeois; and that Hungary offered a military alliance to revolutionary Russia.

Mihály Károlyi watched these and subsequent developments during the spring of 1919 from a suburban villa on the outskirts of Budapest. Warned that he and his family might be in danger, and mindful of István Tisza's fate, he mounted a machine-gun in the hall, facing the front door – but forgot to load it. On 4 July, Károlyi and his family left Budapest for Prague. He did not return to Hungary for 27 years.

This account, which is mainly concerned with the impact on Hungary, and on two of its leaders, of the Paris Peace Conference can accommodate only a brief summary of internal developments under the Kun regime. Since, however, they exerted an important influence on the attitude of the Peace Conference towards what had now become the Hungarian Federal Socialist Republic of Councils, they must be mentioned. During the four months which followed what was, in effect, a bloodless coup, Béla Kun succeeded in imposing on Hungary the complete Leninist agenda of

'We cannot be blind to what has just happened in Hungary. Károlyi was favourable to us and endeavouring to work with us, but found no encouragement ... Result: Hungary is now joining hands with Bolshevist Russia ...'

GENERAL SMUTS TO LLOYD GEORGE, 26 MARCH 1919[4]

expropriation, nationalisation, regimentation and terror. The journalist H N Brailsford wrote in April 1919: '[In the Hungarian press] page after page is filled with "orders" which regulate every phase of life – from the distribution of boots to the repertoire of the theatre.'[5]

Fortunately for the Hungarian people, implementation of the torrent of decrees and ordinances that poured out of the Revolutionary Council was at best patchy, especially outside the capital. Kun was driven by hunger for the approval of his hero and mentor, Lenin; parroting the master, Kun proudly declared: 'I know of no difference between moral and immoral acts: I recognise only one standpoint, whether a thing is good or bad for the proletariat.' [6] In this spirit, the Revolutionary Council nationalised all industrial, mining and transport enterprises, the banks and all private housing. Adult accommodation was limited to one room per head and zealous proletarians were billeted in bourgeois homes to report on the activities of the owners. All estates of more than 100 acres were confiscated without compensation and converted into co-operatives or state farms. The state took over and secularised all schools and universities; the Academy of Sciences was closed down. Rigid censorship tamed the press. Ration cards, without which food could not be legally purchased, were issued only to trade union members. More creditably, the new regime enfranchised all men and women over 18 years of age (but disenfranchised all employers of labour), introduced an eight-hour working day, gave women equality of pay with men and improved the system of unemployment benefit introduced by Károlyi.

For the first few weeks of its existence, the Kun regime enjoyed a honeymoon with the middle as well as the working classes. Kun's proclamations skilfully exploited mounting resentment against Hungary's treatment by the Allies and the public offer of alliance with Bolshevik Russia was seen as a well-deserved rebuff to the Council of Four. But the regime's popularity quickly began to evaporate as economic and social conditions worsened. Inflation, initially fuelled by the Károlyi government's reckless issues of paper money – a policy which Kun continued – spiralled out of control; the peasantry, already alienated by the suspension of Károlyi's distributive land reform, bitterly resented the procurement of food for the towns by armed force. The use of terror to compel obedience and root out suspected disloyalty appalled all classes of the population, including the intelligentsia which had at first welcomed the advent of Communism in Hungary. Tibor Szamuely, nominally Commissar for Education, presided over a 'Red Terror' which claimed nearly 600 lives during the regime's short existence; as in Lenin's Russia, 'defence of the revolution' provided cover for corruption, personal revenge and gratuitous sadism. By the summer of 1919, the Revolutionary Council's credit with the Hungarian people, apart from the radicalised urban working class, was virtually exhausted.

Meanwhile, and from the inception of the Kun regime, the Council of Four in Paris had been watching events in Hungary with mounting concern. True to his promise, Vyx had indeed 'packed his bags' and left Budapest on 26 March; the Belgrade armistice was of course already a dead letter but the departure of the French Military Mission, and of the other Allied missions, formalised the fact. Another significant departure from the capital was that of István Bethlen, who left for Vienna on the day after the Kun take-over, in disguise and with a forged passport. As the leader of the recently formed Party of National Unity, an openly conservative and counter-revolutionary organisation, Bethlen would have been an obvious target for Szamuely's death squads. One of Kun's first acts after issuing the Revolutionary Council's proclamation 'To All' had been to address a Note to the Peace Conference assuring it of the new regime's peaceful intentions: it recognised the armistice; its intended alliance with Russia did not mean that Hungary wished to suspend diplomatic intercourse with the Allies. The Revolutionary Council stood ready to negotiate territorial questions on the basis of the principle of self-determination and would welcome the

6
Dismemberment

The Supreme Council of the Peace Conference had decided at an early stage of its deliberations that the task of drawing up recommendations for the definition of the new frontiers of the defeated powers, in the light of the claims made upon them by the victors, should be delegated to committees of officials of the four principal Allies. The committees would be advised by acknowledged experts on the regions concerned. Hungary could expect no favours from either. On the Romanian and Yugoslav Committee, tasked with considering the claims of those two 'victorious' countries, the junior British representative was Allen Leeper, a talented official with strong Romanian sympathies; while on the Czechoslovak Committee, Britain was represented by Harold Nicholson, who later wrote a brilliant account of the work of the conference, based on his own diaries. Nicholson made no secret of his antipathy to Hungary and Hungarians: 'I confess that I regarded, and still regard, that Turanian tribe with acute distaste. Like their cousins the Turks, they had destroyed much and created nothing ... For centuries the Magyars had oppressed their subject nationalities. The hour of liberation and of retribution was at hand.'[1]

The expert on east-central Europe whom these far-from-neutral British officials consulted most frequently was, of course, Robert Seton-Watson, whose views on Hungary we have already encountered. Nicholson recalled: 'Allen Leeper and myself never moved a yard without previous consultation with experts of the authority of Dr Seton-Watson, who was in Paris at the time.'[2] Wickham Steed, another Magyarphobe, was also in Paris covering the proceedings of the Conference for *The Times*, and was not backward in offering his views and advice to the Committees. These were unhappy auguries for Hungary, who had not been invited to state her own case before the Conference or its committees.

Other factors further reduced the likelihood of objective treatment by the Conference of the question of Hungary's future frontiers. In the first place, the two territorial committees dealing with claims against Hungary drew up their recommendations independently, on the basis of their respective terms of reference; there was thus no monitoring of the *aggregate* impact of their proposals. Harold Nicholson again: 'The Committee on Rumanian Claims, for instance, thought only in terms of Transylvania, the Committee on Czech Claims concentrated upon the southern frontier of Slovakia. It was only too late that it was realised that these two entirely separate Committees had between them imposed upon Hungary a loss of territory and population which, when combined, was very serious indeed.'[3]

This crucial flaw in the structure of the Conference was compounded, moreover, by confusion over the nature of its end-game. When the Conference opened, its participants were under the impression that agreement between the Allies on the terms of a Preliminary Peace Treaty would be followed by a Congress, in which all belligerents and neutral countries would be represented and in which the terms of a Final Peace Treaty would be hammered out in discussion and negotiation. Probably because it postulated a wearisomely long scenario, this concept gradually metamorphosed into that of a single, imposed Final Treaty; the officials working in the territorial committees, however, continued to believe that their recommendations would eventually be submitted to a forum in which all interested parties, including the defeated enemy powers, would have their say. The committees consequently employed the common diplomatic tactic of building into their recommendations 'negotiating fat' – constructing a maximalist position which included elements that could, if necessary, be conceded in negotiation without weakening the essentials. In the event, however, no negotiations took place. The committees' recommendations were consequently embodied in the final text of the Treaty virtually unchanged, with the 'negotiating fat' untrimmed.

There were important differences in the objectives and criteria of the four principal Allies in drawing up their recommendations. The Americans gave priority to the principle

HAROLD NICOLSON ON CONFERENCE PROCEDURES
'We [in the territorial Committees of the Conference] were never for one instant given to suppose that our recommendations were absolutely final. And we thus tended to accept compromises, and even to support decisions, which we ardently hoped would not ... be approved.'

'Had it been known from the outset that no negotiations would ever take place with the enemy, it is certain that many of the less reasonable clauses of the Treaty would never have been inserted'

In making these comments[4] on the procedures of the Peace Conference, Harold Nicolson was referring mainly to the evolution of the Peace Treaty with Germany; but it is clear that the same mind-set governed the drafting of the Treaties with other former enemies, including Hungary.

of ethnicity and tried to ensure that the new frontiers con-
formed as closely as possible to the ethnic map of the regions
concerned; on the whole, this should have been favourable to
Hungary. But the British, infected by Seton-Watson's enthusiasm for nation-making, attached prime importance to the
economic and strategic viability of the new states to whose
birth they were committed – Czechoslovakia, Yugoslavia and
'Greater Romania'. Nicholson noted in his diary for 2 March
1919, a classic example of this difference of approach: '...
Then examine frontier from Komorn [Komárom] to Jung.
The very devil. The Yanks want to go north along the ethni-
cal line, thus cutting all the railways. We want to go south,
keeping the Kassa-Komorn lateral communications, *in spite
of the fact that this will mean putting some 80,000 Magyars
under Czech rule* [emphasis added].'[5]

The French, who were mainly concerned with stemming the
Bolshevik tide but also with maximising their future influence
in the region, tended to support virtually any claim which the
representatives of the new states – or 'successor states' as they
were beginning to be called – cared to put forward. The Italians
were wholly preoccupied with quarrels with the Yugoslavs over
the division of the Balkan spoils and usually went along with
the majority on other issues. The upshot was that the Americans were usually outvoted in committee by three to one, a
pattern wholly inimical to Hungarian interests. But in judging
the work of the Committees it should be borne in mind that
their task was to define the frontiers of the successor states, not
those of Hungary; and that it was inevitable that the interests
of a recent enemy should be subordinated to those of allies.

The Romanians, represented by Prime Minister Ion
Bratianu, elbowed their way into first place in presenting
their claims to the Council of Ten, on 1 February. Bratianu

demanded for Romania the whole of Transylvania together with a broad swathe of Hungarian territory which would take the Romanian frontier up to the river Tisza. As we have seen, he also alleged a Hungarian-Russian plot against Romania which necessitated Allied occupation of a neutralised strip of Hungarian territory to protect his country. Beneš, for Czechoslovakia, followed on 5 February, claiming the whole of Slovakia – which, he alleged with a fine disregard for historical fact, had formed part of a Czechoslovak state before being overrun by the Magyars in the 10th century; he also demanded a corridor, carved out of western Hungary, to link the new Czechoslovakia with Yugoslavia. The Yugoslav delegation presented its claims on 18 February, largely for Hungarian territory which Serbian forces had already occupied: the counties of Baranya and Bácska and half of the Bánát. The guiding consideration in this case was to give the Yugoslav capital, Belgrade, a protective cushion against future aggression from the north.

EYRE CROWE ON FRIENDS AND FOES

'When we come to face these ethnographical difficulties it makes a great difference whether they arise between the Roumanians and the Hungarians, who are our enemies, or between the Roumanians and the Serbs, who are our Allies. In the first case if it were found to be impossible to do justice to both sides, the balance must naturally be inclined toward our ally Roumania rather than toward our enemy Hungary. At the same time this principle must not be carried too far, for our ultimate duty is to produce a condition of things likely to lead to permanent peace.'

Sir Eyre Crowe, senior official in the British delegation[6]

Given the complexity of their task, the two territorial Committees completed their work with remarkable speed. The Czechoslovak Committee submitted its report to the Council on 12 March, only five weeks after its first meeting; it had met only seven times and had heard only one witness – Eduard Beneš. The Romanian and Yugoslav Committee deliberated for a little longer, reporting to the Council on 6 April. During the interval between the submission of the two reports, one powerful voice was raised in warning against over-tidy and over-speedy solutions to the territorial conundrums confronting the Committees – that of the British Prime Minister, David Lloyd George. In his Memorandum dated 25 March and entitled 'Some Considerations for the Peace Conference Before They Finally Draft Their Terms', Lloyd George stressed the long-term dangers of imposing too harsh a peace on Germany and continued: 'What I have said about the Germans is equally true of the Magyars. There will never be peace in South-Eastern Europe if every little state now coming into being is to have a large Magyar Irredenta within its borders. I would therefore take as a guiding principle of the peace that as far as is humanly possible the different races should be allocated to their motherlands, and that this human criterion should have precedence over considerations of strategy or economics or communications, which can usually be adjusted by other means.'[7] This was a remarkable and far-sighted statement, more in line with the United States' negotiating approach than with that of the Prime Minister's own government. To Hungary's, and Europe's, misfortune it was, as we shall see, virtually ignored.

Meanwhile, the first reports had reached the Conference of the Communist take-over in Hungary. At a special meeting of the Council of Four on 25 March to discuss the situation and, in particular, Béla Kun's Note to the Conference, Clemenceau delivered an anti-Hungarian tirade and argued strongly for Allied military intervention; President Wilson and Lloyd George argued against it and this pattern was repeated at a further meeting four days later. As a compromise, the Council decided on 31 March to send the South African Foreign

Minister, General Jan Smuts, on a mission to Budapest, to investigate the situation there and report back. Smuts, one of the architects of the League of Nations, shared both Wilson's idealism and Lloyd George's doubts as to the wisdom of overly punitive peace treaties. He arrived in Budapest by train on 4 April and held two meetings with Kun in his railway carriage which, in order to avoid any suggestion of recognition of the Communist regime, he declined to leave. Smuts renewed the proposal in the Vyx ultimatum for the creation of a neutral zone on Hungarian territory but stressed that the proposed demarcation lines should not be regarded as political frontiers; he offered a modification of the lines favourable to Hungary, moving the Romanians further east, and the lifting of the Allies' economic blockade. In return, Smuts asked that the Hungarian government should confirm that it regarded the Belgrade Armistice as binding and desist from any attempt to re-arm. Kun mistakenly regarded this as the opening bid in a bargaining session. He made acceptance of the Council's offer conditional upon the immediate withdrawal of Romanian troops to the east of the Maros river, in accordance with the Belgrade Armistice terms; and, seeing this as a possible route to the international recognition of his regime, proposed a conference in Prague or Vienna to discuss the whole question of Hungary's frontiers. Smuts refused to modify his offer and concluded, both from his meetings with Kun and from reports made to him by the departing Allied Missions, that Kun was not to be taken seriously and that his regime would not last long. He returned to Paris to report accordingly.

While the Council was considering the Smuts report and a further bleat from Bratianu demanding the complete disarmament of Hungary, the Romanians decided to take matters into their own hands. On 16 April, Romanian troops advanced into Hungary on a broad front between the Szamos and Maros rivers, soon reaching the river Tisza which they crossed on 1 May. There were now no natural obstacles between the Romanian front line and Budapest. The Romanian success encouraged the Czechs to resume their own advance southwards from Miskolc; by 18 May, they threatened the historic town of Eger. Without any intervention from the Peace Conference, Hungary was being torn apart.

The Conference was not, however, idle and its mills ground on. On 31 March, the Council of Four had decided to concentrate its attention on Germany and to delegate lesser matters, including the question of Hungary's future frontiers, to the Council of Five, which consisted of the Foreign Ministers of the four major Allies with the addition of the Foreign Minister of Japan. This junior Council considered the reports of the two territorial Committees (Czechoslovak and Romanian-Yugoslav) at a single meeting on 8 May. The British Foreign Minister, Arthur Balfour, proposed that since the Council could not possibly consider in detail the entire work of the Committees, their reports, which were both unanimous, should be accepted as they stood. This was agreed, although the American Secretary of State, Robert Lansing expressed some doubts. The two reports were therefore submitted, unchanged, to the Council of Four with the recommendation that they should be approved. The minutes of the Council of Four's meeting on 12 May, 1919, baldly state:

'(d) Remaining frontiers of Hungary
After a short statement by M. Tardieu [the French chairman of the Romanian and Yugoslav Committee] the frontiers of Hungary, as laid down in Annexure A, were accepted.
The meeting then adjourned.'[8]

The maximalist recommendations of the two Committees, drafted by relatively junior officials advised by openly anti-Hungarian 'experts', were thus approved at the highest level, without discussion or amendment, within the space of five days.

What was the effect of 'Annexure A'? Its import was to award to Romania the whole of Transylvania, a significant strip of Hungarian territory to the west of the Transylvanian border and the eastern half of the Bánát; to Yugoslavia, all of Croatia/Slavonia, the western half of the Bánát and most of the Bácska; and to Czechoslovakia, all of the predominantly Slovak and Ruthene regions of northern Hungary, plus a strip of Hungarian territory south of the ethnic borderline. A particularly bitter pill for Hungary to swallow was the award to Austria, Hungary's partner in the Austro-Hungarian Monarchy and wartime ally to whom Hungary had remained loyal throughout, of a strip of western Hungary which included the historic Hungarian town of Sopron.

The Austrians, towards whom the Allies seemed remarkably well disposed – unlike Hungary, they had not blotted their copybook by spawning

'This [the award to Austria] was exacted from us at a time when Austria was as much a vanquished nation as we were and, what is more, vanquished in a war into which we had been drawn only because of our connection with Austria, a war that was wanted by no one in Hungary and which had started because an Austrian archduke had been murdered. The ultimatum to Serbia had come from Vienna, and in the royal council that had ordered it the only dissenting voice had been that of István Tisza, prime minister of Hungary.'
MIKLÓS BÁNFFY, AUTHOR AND FOREIGN MINISTER OF HUNGARY, 1921–2[9]

a Communist regime – had argued that the area concerned was populated mainly by ethnic Germans; in coveting a significant agricultural region close to Vienna, they were also exacting revenge for Hungary's refusal, during the war, to allocate to Austria a proportionate share of its food production. The Supreme Council accepted the Austrian claim, making its only award to a defeated nation.

These awards had the following implications: the reduction of Hungary's area by two-thirds; the reduction of Hungary's population by half; the confiscation from Hungary of two-thirds of her railway, road and canal networks, together with about 80 per cent of her forests and mines; and – perhaps more importantly than all these losses – the transfer of over three million ethnic Magyars to Czechoslovak, Romanian, Yugoslav or Austrian rule. These deprivations were massively more severe than those which were to be inflicted, in the Treaty of Versailles, on the Allies' principal foe, Germany.

THE TREATY OF TRIANON, 4 JUNE 1920

The Treaty of Trianon reduced the area of Hungary by two-thirds, from 282,000 square kilometres (discounting Croatia) to 93,000 square kilometres; and her population by over half, from 18.2 million to 7.9 million. The territory awarded to Romania alone was greater in area than the rump of Hungary which remained. Over three million ethnic Magyars were transferred to Czechoslovak, Romanian, Yugoslav or Austrian rule. Hungary lost all her salt, gold, silver, copper, mercury and manganese deposits and most of her oil wells. 97 per cent of her pine and fir forests, 87 per cent of her beech and other deciduous forests and 68 per cent of her oak forests were taken from her, as were all her mountain pastures. Her well-developed processing industries remained but with little grain and no minerals to process. Overall, Hungary retained only 38 per cent of her pre-1914 national wealth.

Hungary, and her temporary rulers, were to remain ignorant of the Council's decisions for a little longer. Hungarian energies, such as remained, were now concentrated on resisting the violations of her territory by her neighbours. Béla

Kun had responded to the renewed Romanian and Czecho-slovak offensives with a swift enlargement of the Red Army (as it was now called), by conscripting all non-commissioned ranks of the former Austro-Hungarian army and accepting the services of the large number of former officers who volunteered to fight the invaders. The socialist Commissar for War, Vilmos Böhm, made a brilliant appointment in making Colonel Aurél Stromfeld, a war veteran and former professor at the Military Academy, his chief of staff and, effectively, commander of the Red Army. Within a few weeks, Stromfeld transformed a demoralised rabble into a disciplined fighting force of 200,000 men, highly motivated in defence of their homeland. On 20 May, the revitalised Red Army launched an offensive towards the north-east which shattered the right flank of the Romanian line and, wheeling left, drove the Czechs out of northern Hungary. By the end of May, the Hungarians had re-captured Kassa (Košice) and occupied a substantial slice of Slovakia, threatening Pozsony (Bratislava).

Hungarian successes in the field, and by a 'Red Army' at that, thoroughly alarmed the Peace Conference in Paris. In the hope, presumably, of stabilising the situation the Council of Four decided to go public with its recent decisions on Hungary's future frontiers. In two telegrams to the Hungarian Revolutionary Council, of which the first was also sent to the Czechoslovaks and Romanians, the four Allies on 13 June spelt out 'the frontiers permanently dividing Hungary from Czechoslovakia and from Roumania', ordered all three states to cease hostilities and to return to within their new frontiers without delay. Hungary was given four days in which to comply; in the event of non-compliance, the Allies reserved the right to occupy Budapest. But the second telegram added a carrot to the stick in the first: as soon as Hungarian troops had evacuated Czechoslovak territory, Romanian troops would be withdrawn from Hungarian territory.

This was a tempting offer and Kun decided to accept it in principle. A Romanian withdrawal could be represented as a victory for his regime and would offset, in propaganda terms, the withdrawal of the Red Army from Slovakia. The recovery of Hungarian territory east of the Tisza would ease a food shortage which was already causing riots in the countryside. Moreover, the forces of counter-revolution were gathering strength, instigating mutinies in the Danube Flotilla and Ludovika Military Academy, and strikes by railwaymen in Sopron and Székesfehérvár. But, fatally, Kun could not resist the temptation to haggle over the details of the Allied offer and did so for several days. Marshal Foch, for the Allies, soon lost patience and on 23 June presented the Revolutionary Council with an ultimatum: if the Red Army had not ceased hostilities within 24 hours, Allied forces or their surrogates would intervene and occupy Budapest. The Council caved in. The Red Army's withdrawal from Slovakia began on 30 June and by 4 July had been completed. The retreat, following so soon after a victorious advance, shattered its morale. Stromfeld resigned in protest. To make matters worse, the Romanians refused to play their allotted role in the bargain and, instead of withdrawing, dug in on the banks of the Tisza. In desperation, Kun ordered his demoralised troops to launch an offensive against the Romanians on a broad front on 20 July. The offensive collapsed after a few days and the Romanians, counter-attacking, crossed the Tisza. The road to Budapest lay open.

On 26 July, the Allies appealed to the Hungarian people over the heads of the Kun regime. In a public statement, they declared that peace and economic recovery would not be possible until Hungary had a government which represented the people and kept its word: 'If food and supplies are to be made available, if the blockade is to be removed, if economic reconstruction is to be attempted, if peace is to be settled it can only be done with a Government which represents the Hungarian people and not with one that rests its authority upon terrorism ... all foreign occupation of Hungarian territory, as defined by the Peace Conference, will cease as soon as the terms of the armistice ... have been satisfactorily complied with.' [10]

With Romanian troops only 100 kilometres from the capital and closing fast, the Revolutionary Council conceded defeat and abdicated in favour of a government of Social Democratic trade unionists headed by Gyula Peidl. Like Napoleon before him and Adolf Hitler later, Kun blamed his failure on his compatriots. In his farewell speech to the Budapest Council of Workers' and Soldiers' Deputies on 1 August, he complained: 'If there had been a class-conscious revolutionary proletariat [in Hungary] then the dictatorship of the proletariat would not have fallen in this way ... Now I see that our experiment to educate the proletarian masses of this country into class-conscious revolutionaries has been in vain. This proletariat needs the most inhumane and cruel dictatorship of the bourgeoisie to become revolutionary.' [11] Later on the same day, Kun and his principal colleagues boarded a train for Vienna, where they had been promised political asylum, and, with the exception of Tibor Szamuely who committed suicide *en route*, eventually reached Moscow. They left behind them a country traumatised by the experience of 133 days of Communism. Despite its brevity, the Kun regime left a profound impression on the Hungarian national psyche. It instilled a hatred of Communism and, by association, a deep hostility to the Soviet Union which, 20 years later, helped to account for Hungary's tolerance of right-wing extremism, apparent indifference to the horrors of Nazism and passive acquiescence in the occupation of Hungary by Nazi Germany. Since the leading figures in the Revolutionary Council had been Jewish, the Kun experience also revived anti-Semitic sentiment in Hungary, which had never been far from the surface.

As Béla Kun and his comrades arrived in Vienna, another group of Hungarians was preparing to leave it.

7
Counter-revolution

Since forming the National Unity Party in February 1919, István Bethlen had become the acknowledged leader of opposition to, firstly, the Károlyi government and then, from Vienna, to Kun's Revolutionary Council. After arriving in Vienna on 24 March, Bethlen concentrated his energies on bringing together into one organisation the various counter-revolutionary groups which had gathered in the Austrian capital. Against the odds, he succeeded and on 12 April was elected chairman of the new Hungarian National Committee – subsequently renamed the 'Anti-Bolshevik Committee' or 'ABC'. The ABC enjoyed the sympathy of the head of the British Military Mission, Colonel Cunninghame, and benefited – at least by his own account[1] – from the active support of a British journalist, Ellis Ashmead-Bartlett, who was covering events in Central Europe for the *Daily Telegraph*. Using Cunninghame as a conduit, the ABC bombarded the Allies with proposals for military intervention against the Kun regime, to be supported by a popular uprising which the ABC undertook to foment, and for raising a Hungarian counter-revolutionary army in the regions occupied by the French and the Serbs. Partly because the Allies had already decided to end their involvement in the civil war in southern Russia, where the White Army faced defeat, these plans commanded no sympathy in Paris; even Clemenceau was now opposed to military action against Kun.

The ABC in any case lacked the financial wherewithal to recruit an army or foment insurrection. Attempts to raise a loan from Austrian banks came to nothing. Then, at the end of April, news reached the ABC that large sums of money had been sent from Budapest to the Hungarian Legation in Vienna to finance subversive activity in Austria and Czechoslovakia, as a first step towards stimulating Communist revolutions in central and then western Europe. With Bethlen's approval, a group of former military officers led by Marquis Pallavicini, an ultra-conservative monarchist, planned to burgle the Legation and appropriate the cash. Taking advantage of the absence of the Hungarian Minister, who had been called to Budapest for consultations, the burglary took place on 2 May. Astonishingly, given the indifferent organisational talents of the counter-revolutionaries, it succeeded and yielded for the ABC's coffers the huge sum of 135 million Hungarian crowns (roughly equivalent to 70 million Swiss francs). The various factions which made up the ABC thereupon began a prolonged squabble over the division of the spoils. The first attempt to make use of these funds ended in farce: elaborate plans to penetrate Hungarian territory from the Austrian border town of Brück, in order to raise western Hungary for the counter-revolutionary cause, collapsed when only a handful of officers turned up at the appointed rendezvous. Moreover, the episode finally exhausted Austrian patience with the ABC's activities; Chancellor Karl Renner approved a recommendation from his Foreign Minister that the group should be expelled. Generally speaking, the conduct of the counter-revolutionary groups in Vienna justified the judgement of the French General Charpé: 'The Hungarians are, as you know, a race of charming children.'[2]

As it happened, Bethlen had already decided that the ABC should transfer its activities to the south-eastern Hungarian town of Szeged, where Count Gyula Károlyi – a cousin of Mihály but his bitter political opponent – had formed a provisional counter-revolutionary government. The obliging Colonel Cunninghame procured Serbian visas (Szeged could be reached only from the south) for about 20 members of the group, who departed from Vienna at the beginning of June. Bethlen decided to remain in Vienna for the time being, as the provisional government's emissary and propagandist. After the collapse of the Kun regime, however, he returned to Budapest on 9 August. He found the capital in chaos and disorder. Romanian troops had marched into the city six days earlier and had immediately embarked on a systematic programme of looting, expropriation, deportations and terror. Having set up their headquarters, the Romanian High Command issued a proclamation inviting active and reserve officers of the former Austro-Hungarian army to present themselves there, and at Romanian army posts in the provinces, in order to assist in the creation of a temporary police force. Several thousand Hungarian officers responded to this appeal. They were immediately arrested, herded into railway wagons and transported to Transylvania as 'prisoners of war', thus eliminating at a stroke the fighting capacity of the Hungarian army.

The Romanian High Command now presented an ultimatum to the Peidl government demanding the immediate delivery to Romania of: military equipment for an army of 300,000;

50 per cent of all Hungary's railway rolling stock; 30 per cent of Hungary's livestock and agricultural machinery; 20,000 wagon-loads of barley and fodder; 50 per cent of all Hungarian shipping; and 400 motor lorries. In addition, Hungary was to dismantle all her munitions factories, release all Romanian prisoners of war, provide coal for the transportation of the expropriated goods and materials and make payment in full for the costs of the Romanian occupation. Only when all these conditions had been fulfilled would a Romanian withdrawal begin. Gyula Peidl's cabinet remained in office only just long enough to take delivery of this ultimatum: on 6 August István Friedrich, a right-wing nationalist businessman, and a group of like-minded conservatives marched into the cabinet room and evicted the Social Democrats who, demoralised, appear to have offered no resistance.

The Romanian ultimatum at last awoke the Supreme Council in Paris to the reality of the maelstrom it had unleashed. Through the Inter-Allied Military Mission which it had despatched to Budapest on 5 August, under the American General Harry Hill Bandholtz, to ensure Hungary's observance of the armistice, the Council conveyed repeated warnings and protests to the Romanian High Command against the excesses of the occupation troops. These were rejected with contumely. The British member of the Mission, General Gorton, reported: 'Harmless individuals are assaulted, food, livestock, agricultural implements and rolling stock are requisitioned and sent to Romania and through the purposeless blockade and destruction of railways, Budapest is on the verge of starvation.'[3] Wholesale looting of the Hungarian National Museum was prevented only by the prompt action of General Bandholtz in taking the Museum under the protection of the Military Mission and sealing its doors.

All over Hungary, the situation was spiralling out of control. The Peace Conference could only wring its hands. Taking advantage of the prevailing confusion, the Czechs occupied part of the designated neutral zone, including the Salgotarján coal mines, in defiance of an Allied protest; in the south, the Yugoslavs advanced across the armistice demarcation line, ignoring an Allied injunction to withdraw. When the new Friedrich government attempted to restore some semblance of constitutionality by installing the Archduke Josef as provisional Regent, Eduard Beneš enlisted the support of the Romanians and Yugoslavs for his hysterical protest: '[The Habsburg] is a Germanic dynasty, it will never be anything else; it is a proud, absolutist and anti-liberal dynasty, the very name of which is hated ... by every Czech.'[4] Bowing to the resulting Allied pressure, Josef resigned, leaving Friedrich to carry on as Prime Minister in a constitutional vacuum. By early September, however, the Supreme Council had begun to worry that if Romania continued to strip Hungary of her economic assets, Hungary would be unable to make the reparations which were to be demanded of her in the eventual peace treaty: it therefore raised its game. On 5 September, the Council decided to send a British diplomat, Sir George Clerk, to Bucharest in an attempt to persuade the Romanian government to call off its marauding troops. He took with him a Declaration from the Council expressing its 'deepest concern' over Romanian behaviour: 'Hungary, suing for peace, already partially disarmed, without allies and without food, has been overrun by troops who, under orders from Bucharest, systematically strip it of every species of moveable wealth, alive or dead, which seems worth the labour of transportation. Cattle, horses, agricultural implements, raw material, machinery, railway equipment, even the outfit of a children's hospital, choke the lines which lead from Buda Pesth [*sic*] to Roumania ... the Associated Powers are reluctantly compelled to ask themselves whether Roumania still counts herself among their number. None of the events that have occurred during the last few weeks are of a nature to reassure them ... Roumania has persistently treated Hungary as a conquered province, and herself as its conqueror, sole and irresponsible. There is no sign that she still deems herself a member of the Alliance, or that in her judgement the Five Great Powers who mainly won the war have any predominant claim to settle the terms of peace.'[5]

In over two weeks of talks with Ion Bratianu, Clerk made no headway whatsoever. General Bandholtz attributed this, perhaps uncharitably, to the wiles and charms of Queen Marie, the most formidable weapon in Romania's diplomatic armoury: 'It was most apparent that Sir George [Clerk], owing to his prolonged stay in Bucharest, had listened to the siren voice of the enchantress Queen, and had fallen under the spell of the Romanian environment. Her Majesty certainly seems to think that she can control any man whom she meets, and it must be admitted that she has considerable foundation for that opinion.'[6]

Far from making any concessions to the Allies, Bratianu even put forward demands for more Hungarian territory. Clerk guessed, correctly, that the Romanian strategy was to acquire as much in the way of foodstuffs as could be transported, far in excess of her own domestic requirements, in order to sell much of it back to the Reparations Commission. Leaving Bucharest empty-handed, Clerk travelled to Budapest to assess the situation there for himself. Just a few days before his arrival, on 13 October, General Bandholtz and his colleagues in the Inter-Allied Military Mission had forwarded to Paris a report prepared by a member of the British Food Commission and a Swiss representative of the International Red Cross after visiting 12 Hungarian towns under Romanian occupation. Their report read, in part: 'In all towns occupied by Roumanians [*sic*] we found an oppression so great as to make life unbearable. Murder is common, youths and women flogged, imprisoned without trial, arrested without reason, theft of personal property under name of requisition ... Experienced Hungarian Directors of Hospitals have been replaced by inexperienced Roumanian doctors. Roumanian military authorities demand petition for every passport, request for coal or food. Petition must be written in Roumanian language, Roumanian lawyer must be employed, and he charges enormous fees ... Roumanians advanced suddenly to Boros-Sebes and two hundred and fifty Hungarian soldiers were taken prisoner. They were killed in most barbarous manner; stripped naked and stabbed with bayonets in a way to prolong life as long as possible.' And much more in the same vein.[7]

After discussions with the Inter-Allied Military Mission and others, Clerk concluded that if matters were to be brought under control, Hungary had to have a government sufficiently representative for the Allies to recognise and with sufficient standing to negotiate with the Romanians. Friedrich and his right-wing colleagues were already working their way down the counter-revolutionary agenda at breakneck speed: Károlyi's land reform had been scrapped, social benefits abolished and supporters of either of the two revolutions dismissed from their posts – on some, death sentences had been passed. From Szeged, Gyula Károlyi endorsed Friedrich's activities and had already unleashed the 'Hungarian National Army' of about 30,000 officers and men, under the command of Admiral Miklós Horthy, in support of the counter-revolution.

While the Romanians were terrorising Budapest and the towns of eastern Hungary, Horthy had led his National Army from Szeged into western Hungary where it initiated a campaign of counter-revolutionary retribution which became known as 'the White Terror'. Armed detachments, led by junior officers, scoured the Hungarian countryside for known or suspected supporters of the Kun regime. Jews were automatically assumed to have Communist sympathies and the pogrom returned to Hungarian towns and villages. In Siófok, on Lake Balaton, over 200 victims were tortured and executed; in Kecskemét, a similar number were flayed or buried alive, some meeting a swifter death by hanging; in a village near Tapolca, Jewish children were flung into wells. Estimates of the toll taken by the White Terror vary widely – from 2,000 to 6,000 lives – but it certainly far exceeded the 'Red Terror' in its ferocity and cruelty.

On 29 October, the Inter-Allied Military Mission summoned the Hungarian Minister of War, General Schnetzer, together with Admiral Horthy and a General in the National Army in order to discuss arrangements for the maintenance of order in the capital following an eventual Romanian withdrawal. General Bandholtz told them that Hungary was about to appear before the Paris Peace Conference; that she was 'to a certain extent discredited' by allowing a Communist regime to exist for three months; that if any disorders arose following a Romanian evacuation, her standing with the Allies would be 'virtually nil'; but if she conducted herself with the dignity of a civilised nation and permitted no serious disorders to arise, she would rise significantly in the Allies' estimation. Bandholtz's account continues: 'I explained to them that there would undoubtedly be some young hot-heads of the Hungarian Army who would be crazy to shoot a Roumanian or hang a Jew, and that one or two such could bring discredit upon the whole country. It was also explained to them that on the part of the workmen of Budapest there existed much fear of the so-called "White Army", and that they should show that their army was not made up of a gang of "White Terrorists", but was a well-disciplined and organised Hungarian National Army. The Admiral said that he had his forces absolutely in hand and under control; that they were well-disciplined and that he would guarantee that there would be no disturbances.'[8]

Both Bandholtz and Clerk were inclined to accept Horthy's assurances. Clerk now concentrated on persuading Prime Minister Friedrich to broaden his government by including in it representatives of the Social Democrats and other parties; he was authorised, he said, to guarantee that such a government would be recognised by the Allies. An invitation to appear before the Peace Conference in Paris would follow. Initially resistant, Friedrich eventually bowed to pressure from both the Allies and from Hungarian party leaders; he agreed to make way for a coalition government, to be led by the Christian Socialist Károly Huszár. It would still be predominantly right-wing in complexion, dominated by the Christian National Unity Party and the Christian Agrarian Labourers' Party; but the Smallholders' Party, the Liberal Party and the Social Democrats would be given one cabinet seat each. In a further success for Clerk and Bandholtz the Romanians, fearful of losing their share of the spoils in Paris if they tried Allied patience further, finally agreed to evacuate Budapest and to withdraw all their troops to the east bank of the river Tisza. Withdrawal from the capital began on 11 November and by 14 November the last Romanian detachment had left Budapest. Advance units of the National Army entered the city a few hours later.

They had begun work on the preparation of their negotiating position under the Károlyi government when Count Pál Teleki, a professor of geography at Budapest University and a talented cartographer, had assembled a team to draw up a demographic map of Hungary showing the distribution of the country's ethnic components. Work came to a halt during the 133 days of the Kun regime but resumed and expanded immediately after its collapse. One of the first acts of the Huszár government was to constitute a delegation to represent Hungary in Paris. Count Albert Apponyi, one of Hungary's leading conservative elder statesmen, was appointed to lead it. Now 73 years of age and patriarchal in appearance, Apponyi had twice held the post of Minister of Education and Religious Affairs in pre-war governments and was the author of the notorious 'Lex Apponyi' of 1907, regarded by Hungary's ethnic minorities as a principal instrument of 'Magyarisation'. He had nevertheless done a great deal to increase the provision of free primary education throughout Hungary and to improve its quality. Head of one of the country's oldest and most respected families, deeply religious and fervently patriotic, Apponyi quintessentially represented 'old Hungary'. He accepted the leadership of his country's peace delegation with a heavy heart: 'I could not refuse this saddest of duties', he recalled in his memoirs, 'though I had no illusions as to there being any possibility of my securing some mitigation of our lot.'[1] The delegation's negotiating strategy would be to hold out for the preservation of Hungary's territorial integrity; but to accept, if necessary, plebiscites in disputed regions in accordance with the Wilsonian principle of self-determination. Two weeks before leaving for Paris with his delegation, Apponyi was a victim of the petty spite which characterised the conduct of the 'successor states' towards Hungary: the Czech authorities denied him permission to spend Christmas with his family on their estate near Pozsony (Bratislava), within the zone occupied by Czechoslovak troops.

Apponyi's delegation included two other prominent conservative politicians: Pál Teleki (the cartographer) and István Bethlen. Teleki, in exile during the Kun period, had held the post of Foreign Minister in Gyula Károlyi's Szeged 'government'; like Bethlen, he would before long become Prime Minister of Hungary. Among the delegation's 73 members were three future Foreign Ministers, the former Governor of the Austro-Hungarian National Bank and a strong team of military, legal and economic experts. As their special train, cobbled together from the wreckage of Hungary's railways, slowly made its way through western Hungary on 5 January 1920, subdued crowds assembled on the platforms of every station to sing the national anthem, wish the delegation well and wave it on its way. At the last station before the Austrian border, the mayor of Sopron delivered a speech urging Count Apponyi to tell the Peace Conference of the warm attachment of the ethnic Germans of western Hungary to their Hungarian motherland. Two days later, the train pulled into a deserted railway station in Paris where it was met by a Military Commission charged with the delegation's custody. From the outset, the cold, formal courtesy extended to the Hungarians was designed to emphasise their status as representatives of a defeated country. Escorted to the Hotel Madrid in the suburb of Neuilly, near the Bois de Boulogne, they were informed that they could not leave it, except for recreational strolls in the Bois, without permission; contact with personal friends in the French capital was forbidden except by special dispensation. Interviews with journalists could be given only with Clemenceau's personal consent. Apponyi's request to establish contact with the American Ambassador, now the sole representative of his country in Paris – the entire United States delegation having left for home in December – was brusquely refused. When the delegation was required to submit its credentials for inspection by the Supreme Council, Apponyi asked, in accordance with normal diplomatic protocol, for a reciprocal inspection of Allied credentials; this request, too, was contemptuously rejected by Clemenceau himself, although the necessary documents were produced at the very last moment. The delegation was invited to present itself before the Supreme Council on 15 January in order to receive the terms on which peace was to be concluded.

Apponyi now seized the first opportunity given to Hungary to set out her case before the Allied powers. This was done in a series of Notes, already prepared in Budapest, setting out the historical grounds for Hungary's appeal against dismemberment and describing her present parlous situation. The Note dealing with Transylvania, drafted by István Bethlen, offered a plebiscite to determine the region's future and its possible division into semi-autonomous ethnic districts – Hungarian, Saxon and Romanian – under a trilingual central administration; its references to the economic and cultural superiority of the Hungarian element of the population over the Romanian, however justified by the facts, were tactically inept. Appended to the Notes, in addition to numerous statistical tables and maps, were copies of István Tisza's memoranda to Emperor Franz Josef in July 1914, opposing the ultimatum to Serbia which had brought war to Europe.

In submitting this material to the Supreme Council on the morning of 15 January, the delegation appealed for a proper hearing before final decisions were taken which could amount to the destruction of the Hungarian state. Later on the same day, at 4 p.m., the delegation gathered in the Red Salon of the Quai d'Orsay; a draft treaty of peace was handed to Count Apponyi by an official while Clemenceau, Lloyd George and representatives of Italy and Japan looked on. Clemenceau then announced that the Supreme Council had decided to grant Apponyi's request for a hearing; he could make a statement before the Council on a date to be agreed. Apponyi replied that he had in mind, not a statement, but a discussion; and requested two days' grace in which to study the terms which had been handed over. Clemenceau thereupon ruled that Apponyi should make his statement on the following day, 16 January, allowing the Hungarians less than 24 hours in which to study the Allied peace terms and prepare Apponyi's response.

The draft peace treaty, feverishly studied by the Hungarian delegation back at their hotel, confirmed their worst fears. The frontiers laid down were precisely as defined in 'Annexure A' to the record of the Council of Four's meeting on 12 May 1919, eight months earlier. In addition, the draft treaty forbade Hungary's reunion with Austria; demanded the protection of the rights of Hungary's minorities, including education in their mother tongue; limited Hungary's army to 35,000 men and proscribed general conscription; forbade the manufacture or purchase of military vehicles, including tanks, naval vessels or military aircraft; confiscated Hungary's Danube Fleet; and imposed reparations, to be determined by the Reparations Commission, which were to paid over a period of 30 years from 1921.

At 3 o'clock on the afternoon of 16 January Apponyi and the leading members of his delegation appeared before Clemenceau, Lloyd George and the new Italian Prime Minister,

Francesco Nitti, at the Quai d'Orsay; the United States was represented by the American Ambassador, Henry Wallace, and the Japanese Ambassador was also present. Apponyi recalled: 'I was to address an audience among whom there was not the slightest sympathetic element, an audience of enemies in the technical sense of the word, and for the most part of men ill-disposed towards us, with a slight admixture of indifferent listeners.'[2]

Invited by Clemenceau to be seated, Apponyi chose to stand. He spoke from notes, in fluent French. After ten minutes, Clemenceau interrupted to say that the speech would now be translated into English. In order to not to lose his flow, Apponyi offered to make the translation himself and did so. From then on, he delivered each section of his speech in French followed by English and at its conclusion delivered a full summary in excellent Italian, to Nitti's evident grati-fication. Apponyi maintained eye contact with his listen-ers throughout; by his own account, Clemenceau's initially hostile, sceptical expression gradually softened. Apponyi began by making it clear that the terms proposed could not be accepted without substantial modification; their acceptance would amount to national suicide. The peace treaties already concluded with Germany, Austria and Bulgaria did not contain territorial changes of anything like the same magni-tude. He demonstrated that the territorial clauses of the draft treaty were wholly misconceived and violated the principle of nationality which the Conference professed to be defending. But if the Conference refused to accept the historical, geo-graphical, economic and cultural arguments for maintaining Hungary's territorial integrity – arguments which Apponyi developed at some length – Hungary would accept plebi-scites: 'In the name of the grand principle formulated with such eloquence by President Wilson, according to which no human group, no part of the population of any state should be placed, like cattle, under the jurisdiction of a foreign state without its consent; in the name of this spirit which, moreover, is an axiom of common sense and public morality, we demand plebiscites in those areas of our country which they want to take away from us. I declare that we will comply with the results of the plebiscite, no matter what the outcome.'[3]

Apponyi argued that the impact of occupation by her neighbours, together with the effects of the Allied economic blockade, had destroyed any possibility of Hungary being able to implement the financial and economic clauses of the draft treaty. He repeated that the proposed loss of two-thirds of Hungary's territory and the transfer of over one-third of the Magyar people to alien sovereignties was a punishment without historical precedent.

When Apponyi had concluded his statement Lloyd George, probably with the intention of initiating a discussion in the area most likely to be helpful to the Hungarian case, asked Apponyi for more details of the numbers and locations of the Magyars who would find themselves outside Hungary; would they be spread along the new frontiers or would they form compact groups? Apponyi seized this opportunity to produce Pál Teleki's demographic map, on which the new borders had been hastily drawn that morning, to show that the Hungarians affected would be both in groups and spread along the frontiers. As he spread the map out on a table, the Allied leaders clustered round to look at it; the atmosphere at once became less formal and more relaxed. Apponyi claims in his memoirs that Lloyd George whispered congratulations on his eloquence; Lloyd George, however, in his recollections, criticised Apponyi for attacking the treaty's terms on too broad a front, indeed questioning its very basis, instead of concentrating on the detail of the new frontiers, where he might have secured some concessions. In closing the session, Clemenceau politely agreed to Apponyi's request for four weeks' grace in which to prepare Hungary's written response to the draft treaty. This was one of his last acts as Prime Minister of France: on the following day, 17 January, Paul Deschanel was elected to the Presidency and appointed Alexandre Millerand to the premiership. Millerand automatically assumed the Chairmanship of the Supreme Council.

On 18 January Apponyi and most members of the Hungarian delegation packed their bags and left by train for Budapest. They left behind a small rearguard, led by István Bethlen, charged with doing everything possible to win the sympathies of the remaining Allied representatives, especially the British. Count Miklós Bánffy had already been sent to London, where he had a number of influential friends, to perform a similar function in British political circles. Apponyi's train drew into Budapest's Western railway station on 20 January, where a large, silent crowd awaited it. The peace terms had been published in the Hungarian press that morning. The railway station, like all the capital's principal buildings and streets, was draped with black flags in mourning for a dismembered country. Apponyi thought this to be a tactical error and, addressing journalists at the station, said so: 'It is my duty, fully aware of my responsibility, to point out that it was premature to fly the black flags of mourning, to decorate our flag with black veils ... We were presented with peace conditions which – again fully aware of my responsibility – I declare in front of the Allied powers, that unless they are substantially modified, are unacceptable to Hungary. But we were asked to present our counter-arguments. And once we were able to break through the isolation surrounding us and managed to speak out, the president of the Council of Five assured me that what I have said, and what we will demonstrate by the documents presented to them will become the subject of careful consideration.'[4]

After delivering a formal report to Admiral Horthy, as acting head of state, Apponyi, Teleki and their team of experts got down to work on the preparation of a detailed critique of the peace treaty, in the form of a series of 18 Notes, with lengthy attachments, dealing with its various sections. Armed with these, the delegation returned to Paris on 9 February and delivered them to the Conference. In all essentials, the Notes consisted of an elaboration of Apponyi's statement on 16 January: re-assertion of Hungary's historic territorial integrity but readiness to concede plebiscites, and to abide by their results, coupled with a host of specific requests for amendments to the peace terms. The Supreme Council of the Peace Conference had held its last meeting on 21 January, following the coming into effect of the Treaty of Versailles; the Council's functions had been transferred to two bodies – the Council of Ambassadors and Foreign Ministers, which met in Paris, and the Council of Heads of Delegation, which met in London. While it awaited a reaction from the Conference to its Notes, the Hungarian delegation continued to be confined to its quarters in Neuilly under conditions of virtual internment. Apponyi's request for the opportunity to make a further oral presentation was rejected; Apponyi and most members of his team consequently returned to Budapest at the end of February, again leaving István Bethlen and a few others to hold the fort.

Meanwhile, Miklós Bánffy had been active in London and to good effect. Mobilising all his personal contacts, he stimulated the airing of the Hungarian question in both Houses of Parliament. Sir Donald Maclean raised the matter in the House of Commons on 12 February, arguing that 'the whole matter [of Hungary's frontiers] should be at once investigated by an impartial Commission of experts and the Treaty finally settled after considering the report of such Commission'.[5] In the House of Lords, Viscount Bryce and Lord Newton also spoke up for Hungary, the latter claiming that 'in some respects Hungary seems to have suffered more than any other country that participated in the war ... Hungary never wanted war'.[6]

These parliamentary interventions may have influenced the attitude adopted by British ministers in meetings of the Council of Heads of Delegation in February and March. At the Council's meeting on 25 February the Foreign Secretary, Lord Curzon, argued that the Hungarian response to the draft treaty could not be ignored: the territorial and economic issues raised in the Hungarian Notes should be discussed by the three Allied leaders and more detailed matters referred to the Council of Ambassadors in Paris. In the same vein, Lloyd George supported a thorough examination of the Hungarian case at the highest level: 'The Allies did not want the Hungarians always to remain hostile, but that would probably happen should the Allies point blank reject (without consideration) Hungary's appeal.'[8] Lloyd George developed his argument further at the Council's meeting on 3 March, pointing out that the treaty left one-third of the total Magyar population of Hungary under foreign rule, a situation which it would not be easy to defend: there would be no peace in Central Europe 'if it

'A settlement that is made in contradiction of the principles of justice will not be a permanent settlement.'

VISCOUNT BRYCE, IN THE HOUSE OF LORDS, 30 MARCH 1920[7]

were discovered afterwards that the claims of Hungary were sound and that a whole community of Magyars had been handed over like cattle to Czechoslovakia and to Transylvania [*sic* – he meant Romania], simply because the Conference had refused to examine the Hungarian case.'[9]

At both meetings, British arguments were supported by the Italian Prime Minister, Nitti, on whom Apponyi's address on 16 January had made – as he confessed in his memoirs – a deep impression. And at both meetings the French representatives, Millerand and Berthelot, adamantly opposed any consideration of amendment to either the territorial or the financial provisions of the treaty. On 3 March, Millerand referred to the Hungarians as 'a most treacherous people' whose statistics 'were notoriously unreliable'; the peace treaty had been agreed by the Conference at all levels and should not be re-negotiated in any respect. The British and Italian leaders could secure agreement to no more than the referral of the whole issue to the Council of Ambassadors and Foreign Ministers.

To the further misfortune of Hungary this lower Council, when it met on 8 March, had before it a memorandum from the British Foreign Office drafted by none other than Allen Leeper, the Magyarphobic official who had promoted Romania's claim to Transylvania in the Romanian and Yugoslav territorial committee of the Peace Conference a year earlier. Predictably, the memorandum argued strongly, even passionately, against any suggestion of amendment to the territorial clauses of the peace treaty: 'If the Supreme Council were now to go back on the decisions they publicly announced to these Governments [of Romania, Yugoslavia and Czechoslovakia] they would be considered everywhere in these countries to have been guilty of a serious breach of faith.

They would find that in return these Governments consider themselves as no longer bound by all the various Treaties concerning minorities and other matters which have been concluded on the basis of the frontiers given in the Peace Treaty.' [10]

Curiously, in view of the stand he had taken in London and given his awareness of Lloyd George's position, Lord Curzon had not only tabled Leeper's memorandum without comment but now proposed that the Council should approve it. He doubtless perceived that the French were immoveable. Anxious, like everybody else except the Hungarians, to conclude the work of the Conference, Curzon decided to settle for what little he and the Italians could get. This was the Council's agreement that if the Frontier Delimitations Commission – the body appointed to supervise the implementation of the frontier changes on the ground – 'found after due enquiry on the spot that in certain areas injustice had been done and modifications were required, they should be at liberty to report their conclusions to the League of Nations'. The French accepted this only with the condition that 'the broad lines of the frontier as fixed in the Treaty … must stand', thus fatally weakening the compromise. [11]

Since the Allies had now, in effect, decided to take no notice of the Hungarian Notes commenting on the terms of the draft peace treaty, there appeared to be no reason for further delay in pressing matters to a final conclusion. But the French, of all people, were now dragging their feet. The reason was that the new Permanent Under-Secretary at the Quai d'Orsay, Maurice Paléologue, and three Hungarian businessmen with French connections were exploring the possibility of concluding a deal whereby French interests would secure a commanding position in the Hungarian economy in return for the French government's support for Hungary's requests for the revision of the peace treaty's territorial provisions. Paléologue and a few of his subordinate officials in the Quai were attracted by the prospect of brokering a settlement of the differences between the countries of East-Central Europe and establishing French dominance of the resulting coherent bloc of small nations. The Hungarians, for their part, were willing to consider offering to France a lease on the entire Hungarian railway system, the contract to construct a commercial port in Budapest and a controlling interest in the Hungarian Credit Bank, which held a majority share in several leading industrial enterprises. The key question, which István Bethlen and his colleague Count Imre Csáky were now authorised by their government to explore, was that of whether, in return for economic concessions of this kind, the French would really adopt a more flexible attitude towards some modification of the territorial clauses of the peace treaty. Hungarians have a remarkable capacity for wishful thinking – perhaps a product of the fact that at so many junctures in their history it seemed incredible that matters could get any worse; and for a brief period hopes ran high in Budapest, both within the government and in the National Assembly, that the French would deliver. Bethlen, however, even as he transmitted to Paléologue a list of Hungary's territorial requirements, kept his feet on the ground; and it came as no surprise to him when Paléologue confirmed, at the beginning of May, that there could be no substantive negotiation until Hungary had signed the peace treaty as it stood. Csáky reported to Budapest: 'The French government could in no wise justify to its allies further delays of the final peace articles.' [12] Paléologue had simply been stringing the Hungarians along on the off-chance of winning a cheap trick for France. No negotiations

The letter went on to confirm that the Delimitation Commission would be authorised to report instances of injustice to the League of Nations. The rights of Magyars transferred to a different sovereignty would be fully protected by the terms of the treaties already concluded with Romania, Yugoslavia and Czechoslovakia. Hungary's fidelity in fulfilling the obligations imposed upon her by the Peace Treaty would bring closer the time at which she might be received into the League of Nations herself. But the provision of authority to the Delimitation Commission to report injustices marked the limit of Allied concessions; there could be no more. 'The Conditions of Peace handed to you this day are, therefore, definitive.' The Hungarian delegation was given ten days to confirm that they had been authorised to sign the treaty as it stood.

Publication of the 'Millerand Letter' in the Hungarian press and its subsequent debate in the National Assembly unleashed a storm of anger and protest in Hungary. Influential voices were raised against signature of the treaty. The leading Budapest daily, *Pesti Hírlap*, proclaimed: 'We cannot sign this treaty ... because we cannot give away the territory of Hungary. No, no, never!' – thus coining, in those last three words, the slogan of revisionism,* '*Nem, nem, soha!*'. Apponyi, however, felt bound to bring the protesters down to earth, telling the national Assembly on 26 May: 'Not signing, which would certainly correspond to justice, to the moral point of view, to the feelings of the nation and to my own feelings, would bring us into conflict with the entire world ...

---

*In this and subsequent chapters, the word 'revision', and its derivatives 'revisionism' and 'revisionist', are shorthand for the aspiration to revise the Treaty of Trianon and for those who espoused this cause.

Such an all or nothing gamble would be taking an inordinate risk with the most treasured possessions of the nation, the rebirth of the nation, the hopes of recovery.' [15]

Supported by Bethlen, Teleki, Csáky and all the senior members of his delegation, Apponyi recommended to his government that the treaty should be signed. This recommendation was accepted by the cabinet and on 18 May Admiral Horthy, in a letter to Millerand, confirmed that, while sharing all the objections to the treaty raised by its delegation in Paris, the Hungarian government had no choice but to sign it. Apponyi and his delegation thereupon resigned in acknowledgement of their failure to secure mitigation of the conditions of peace. The act of signature was entrusted to two men who, lacking further political ambition, were willing to accept the consequent stigma: the Minister for Public Welfare and Labour, Ágoston Benárd, and a career diplomat, Alfred Drasche-Lázár. The two men and their supporting officials arrived in Paris by train on 3 June, the eve of the day appointed by Millerand for signature.

At 4.15 p.m. on 4 June 1920, the Hungarian delegation arrived at the Grand Trianon Pavilion in the grounds of the Palace of Versailles, the location designated by the French Prime Minister, as Chairman of the Council of Heads of Delegation, for the signing ceremony. Millerand and representatives of all the Allied and Associated Powers, awaited them. When the two Hungarians had signed the Treaty, those representing the five major Allies and the other Conference participants followed suit. The Hungarian delegation thereupon withdrew, leaving the Romanian, Czechoslovak and Yugoslav representatives to indulge in an orgy of self-congratulation on their supporting roles in the dismemberment of Hungary. The ceremony had lasted just over 15 minutes.

Count Mihály Károlyi in exile, 1925.

III
The Legacy

9

Bethlen – Consolidation and Recovery

June 4th 1920 was a day of national mourning in Hungary. Budapest was once again draped in black. Newspapers appeared with black borders. Most shops were closed, as were schools and offices. Flags were lowered to half-mast, and on government buildings were to remain so until 1938. Crowds assembled on Heroes' Square to sing the national anthem, whose melancholy falling cadences suited the occasion, and the 'Kossuth song' of national resistance. With black banners bearing the names of the lost territories and the slogan '*Nem, nem, soha!*' the crowds moved slowly down Andrássy Avenue to gather round the statue of the national poet, Sándor Petőfi, on the Pest embankment of the Danube; and then across the Chain Bridge to the Coronation Church, the Mátyás Templom, on Castle Hill, where Mass was to be celebrated. Both in the capital and throughout Hungary, church bells tolled, buses and trains came to a halt and Hungarians stood in silence for five minutes. When the Mass, and parallel services in the principal Protestant churches, were over, the National Assembly met for a brief session.

Addressing the peoples of the 'lost' territories, the Speaker of the House declared: 'From this moment, all our thoughts, all our heartbeats night and day will be directed at reuniting with you in our former glory, our former greatness.'[1]

Anger, grief and humiliation combined to unleash a passionate invocation of the national myth, in which emotion overrode historical reality. In the National Assembly on 5 June, a representative of Hungary's leading national associations set the tone: 'The ancient empire of St Stephen has always been the home of freedom, of right, of order and culture, in which all nations could evolve freely and all individuals could attain happiness according to their merits ... It was the Hungarian nation that gave the continent its first free constitution, it was this nation which defended Europe against Eastern barbarism over the centuries, it was this nation which presented humanity with great and holy rulers, glorious military

> 'The eternal brotherhood and sisterhood of twenty million people of the country of the Hungarians protests against what happened today at the Grand Trianon under the guise of peace. The Hungarian cry of anguish can be heard throughout the unfeeling world and the future harkens to the word of approaching victory of justice as yet unheard.'
> *NEMZETI ÚJSÁG* [*NATIONAL NEWS*], 4 JUNE 1920[3]

leaders, self-sacrificing heroes of liberty, world famous statesmen, a long line of immortal scientists, poets and artists.'[2]

This theme was echoed in every newspaper, irrespective of its political leaning. The Social Democratic daily *Népszava* saw the Peace Treaty as the product of 'blood-soaked clouds of revenge'. *Pesti Napló* proclaimed 'that the peace forced upon us is no peace, that it means not life but a dishonourable death'; but 'the jewel in the crown of St Stephen will shine again …'. *Nemzeti Újság* lamented that 'Europe, which we have defended for a thousand years against the affronts of the barbarian East, has ignominiously affronted us.' During the weeks and months that followed, politicians and publicists clutched at every straw which could be used as evidence of the possibility of early revision of the treaty.

The public mood of anger and defiance in Hungary provided one of the stimuli for the conclusion, on 14 August, of a treaty of alliance between Czechoslovakia and Yugoslavia which provided for mutual assistance if either country were to be attacked by Hungary. Similar treaties were to be concluded in the following year between Romania and Czechoslovakia and between Romania and Yugoslavia, thus completing the network of alliances, known as the Little Entente, between all but one (Austria) of Hungary's neighbours. Meanwhile, the first such alliance had helped to concentrate Hungarian minds on the realities of their country's situation: Hungary was simply in no position to defy the other signatories of the Treaty of Trianon, who were becoming impatient for Hungary's ratification. This was eventually forthcoming on 15 November, after a stormy debate in the National Assembly in which Pál Teleki's appeal, as Prime Minister, for acceptance of the inevitable finally prevailed. Signature of the Treaty by the Regent, Miklós Horthy, completed the process.

Horthy had been elected to the Regency on 1 March 1920, following agreement between the main political parties that, in order to preserve constitutional continuity, Hungary should remain a monarchy – but, for the time being, without a monarch. This compromise between the legitimists, who remained loyal to Charles IV, and the 'free electors', who favoured a break with the Habsburgs and freedom for the National Assembly to choose a sovereign, owed something to a pre-emptive strike by the Allied Powers during the Paris Peace Conference. At the instigation of Beneš, whose loathing of the Habsburgs and all their works was legendary, the Allies informed the Hungarian delegation to the Conference that 'the restoration of a dynasty personifying, in the eyes of their subjects, a system of oppression and domination of other races, in alliance with Germany, would not be compatible with the principles for which they fought nor with the results the war has allowed them to achieve in the liberation of peoples bound hitherto to servitude; … a restoration of this kind … would be neither acknowledged nor tolerated by them.'[4]

A Regency offered the neatest solution to the constitutional dilemma and one to which the Allies could not reasonably object. Miklós Horthy, commander of the National Army and already *de facto* head of state, was the obvious choice for election to an office for which there were respectable precedents in Hungary's history. Aged 52 in 1920, Horthy had enjoyed a naval career of considerable distinction, which had included five years as an aide-de-camp to Emperor Franz Josef and ended with promotion to be commander-in-chief of the Imperial Navy. He was good-looking, with an impressive physical presence and great charm of manner. Horthy was not a clever man but had a remarkable talent for languages; and his personal qualities of honesty, straightforwardness, devotion to family and modesty of lifestyle would be assets in a head of state. There were, of course, flaws as well as virtues. His nationalism, perfervid and blinkered even by Hungarian standards, blinded Horthy to the possibility of shortcomings, past or present, in the conduct of his fellow Hungarians. Loyalty to his own class – his family belonged to the lesser nobility – led him to condone the appalling crimes committed by bands of officers during the White Terror; and his bitter hatred of the political left prompted him, only a fortnight before his election to the Regency, to protect from justice an officer who had murdered the editor of *Népszava*, the Social Democratic newspaper, and one of its journalists. As with many of Horthy's contemporaries, anti-Semitism went hand in hand with his anti-Bolshevism; but it was not pronounced. He enjoyed the company of rich, assimilated Jews whom he regarded as honorary Magyar gentry. Miklós Horthy was usually decent, sometimes stupid, rarely wicked; he was a true conservative, determined to restore the pre-revolutionary *status quo* and to arrest further change.

Both of Albert Apponyi's deputies in the Hungarian peace delegation, Counts Pál Teleki and István Bethlen, became Prime Ministers of Hungary soon after the signature of the Peace Treaty. Teleki's tenure of the office was brief. He mishandled the crisis resulting from the first of Charles IV's two unsuccessful attempts, in 1921, to reclaim the Hungarian Crown,[5] allowing himself to be persuaded by his former sovereign to publish a royalist manifesto in return for Charles's withdrawal. This cost Teleki the premiership; Horthy appointed István Bethlen to replace him. It thus fell to Bethlen to ensure the failure of Charles's second and more determined foray, in October, and subsequently to settle the issue for good by steering through the National Assembly a law which deposed the Habsburg dynasty. The Hungarian throne remained vacant and the Regency came to be accepted as a permanent institution.

Bethlen was at the same time coping with a separate crisis, resulting from the award to Austria, in the Treaty of Trianon, of a strip of western Hungary, the Burgenland. This was a highly sensitive political issue on which the Hungarian

CHARLES IV'S ILL-FATED ATTEMPTS TO REGAIN THE HUNGARIAN THRONE
In June 1920, Charles IV sent two letters to Admiral Horthy, from Switzerland, announcing his intention of returning to Hungary to reclaim his throne. Horthy ignored them. Charles nevertheless arrived in western Hungary in April, 1921, travelled to Budapest with an entourage of Hungarian legitimists (supporters of the Habsburg dynasty) and confronted Horthy. Conscious of the nation-wide tide of anti-Habsburg sentiment, Horthy, unmoved by Charles's promises of high honours and threats of indictment for treason, advised him to return to Switzerland forthwith; Charles eventually did so, leaving behind him a manifesto which Prime Minister Pál Teleki foolishly released to the press. Six months later, however, the former King made a second and more serious attempt. Accompanied by Empress Zita, Charles raised a small army of legitimist supporters in western Hungary and marched on Budapest, reaching the suburbs on 23 October. The new Prime Minister, István Bethlen, persuaded the commander of Charles's small force to change sides and. after an inconclusive skirmish, an armistice was agreed. After spending a week under house arrest, Charles and Zita embarked in Budapest on the British river monitor *Glow-worm* and sailed down the Danube into exile. A week later, the Hungarian Parliament formally deposed the Habsburg dynasty. Charles died in 1922, in Madeira, at the age of 34; Zita, who did not remarry, survived him for 67 years, dying in Switzerland in 1989 at the age of 96.

government had to be seen by Hungarians to be recalcitrant rather than compliant. As Bethlen's Foreign Minister, Count Miklós Bánffy, later recalled: 'The worst of it was that Sopron and its surrounding territory had to be handed over not to one of the victorious powers but to Austria. Not only was this deeply humiliating but in it there was also a diabolical irony. For centuries Hungarians had fought successfully to defend Hungarian land from Austria; but now, when the Allies had broken up the Austrian Empire, it was demanded of us that we should surrender to Austria land that had always been ours.'[6]

Hungary had been required by the Allied powers to withdraw her troops from the Burgenland by the end of August 1921. The withdrawal was begun but Bethlen declined to complete it until Austria had offered guarantees of compensation to the Hungarian owners of the estates and industrial enterprises affected by the transfer. Moreover, the area from which regular Hungarian forces had withdrawn was immediately re-occupied by a volunteer militia led by right-wing officers acting with Bethlen's tacit blessing. Armed clashes occurred between the Hungarian militiamen and Austrian police. Bethlen made it clear to the Allies that, although he would do his best to curb the unofficial militia, he would be unable to control them if the territorial award to Austria was not reduced by at least 20 per cent. Although Austria refused to accept any reduction whatsoever, the Allies, now belatedly conscious of the injustices of Trianon and of this provision in particular, pressured Vienna into acceptance of a plebiscite in Sopron and its immediate vicinity. On Horthy's orders, the militiamen reluctantly withdrew and the plebiscite took place on 14 December 1921. In a high turnout, 65 per cent of the population of the area concerned voted to remain in Hungary – in Sopron itself, the figure was nearly 73 per cent. Despite Austrian protests, this outcome was accepted by the Allied authorities and the transfer of population to Austria reduced by 55,000 Burgenlanders, most of them citizens of Sopron. The Hungarian National Assembly subsequently awarded Sopron the title 'Most Loyal City'. Bethlen had emerged from his first solo international encounter with considerable credit.

The contrast between István Bethlen's rising fortunes and those of Count Mihály Károlyi, whose last appearance in this account marked his departure from Hungary in July 1919,

Europe 1923

FINLAND

Petrograd (St Petersburg)

Tallinn
ESTONIA

Riga
LATVIA

LITHUANIA

Vilnius

Königsberg
EAST
PRUSSIA

Moscow

UNION OF SOVIET
SOCIALIST REPUBLICS

Warsaw ○ Brest-Litovsk

POLAND

Kiev

AKIA

Budapest

ARY

Odessa

ROMANIA

Belgrade ○ Bucharest

SLAVIA

BULGARIA
○ Sofia

Black Sea

NIA

Istanbul

GREECE

TURKEY

Athens

IRAQ

SYRIA

CYPRUS

could hardly have been greater. Since leaving their homeland, with few material assets, Károlyi and his family had been living, in very straitened circumstances, first in Prague and then in Moravia, where they would have read of the Paris negotiations and their outcome. Károlyi's reaction to the terms imposed in the Trianon Treaty is not recorded; but his subsequent career suggests that he probably did not share the bitter anger of most of his countrymen. He is likely to have shared the view expressed in the 'Millerand Letter', that Hungary was being justly punished for past misdeeds and should buckle down to making the best of the new situation.

In this, as in virtually all matters, Bethlen's views were diametrically opposed to Károlyi's: he was determined to work for the revision of Trianon and for the removal of the injustice imposed upon Hungary. But he was also a pragmatist; and his experience of the negotiations in Paris, such as they were, had instilled in him a hard-headed realism which for the next ten years would serve his country well. Bethlen realised that if Hungary was to have any hope of recovering her lost territories, she had first to regain the confidence of the international community by giving evidence of political stability; and then embark on the long, painful process of economic recovery, despite the handicaps imposed by Trianon. In laying the ghosts of revolution and Communism, Bethlen's methods were not pretty; but they were certainly effective. He began by merging the two existing conservative political groupings, the Smallholders and Christian Unity Parties, into a new Unity Party; this, on the pattern established before the war by Kálmán and István Tisza, he moulded into a permanent machine of government, packing it with civil servants and installing its members in key posts in county administration.

Through a succession of unscrupulous political manoeuvres, Bethlen then secured the Unity Party's hegemony by replacing the franchise law of 1920 with the old, more restrictive franchise introduced in 1913. This reduced the proportion of the Hungarian population entitled to vote from 58.4 per cent, under the 'Károlyi franchise', to 28.4 per cent; under the same decree, the secret ballot was abolished in two-thirds of Hungary's parliamentary constituencies – an extraordinarily regressive measure which exposed a majority of the electorate, mostly in the countryside, to the coercion and corruption inseparable from open voting. With breathtaking cynicism, Bethlen remarked that the secret ballot 'was not compatible with the Hungarian people's open character'.

The elections of 1926, in which the Unity Party won 177 out of 245 seats in the national Assembly, confirmed Bethlen's political dominance. This was further enhanced by his revival of an unelected Upper House of the National Assembly, a natural bastion of conservatism and reaction. Meanwhile, Bethlen had been working to ensure that political stability in Hungary would be accompanied by economic recovery. The

'Real democracy grants a leading role to the educated and cultured element. Any political system that tries to negate this principle does not deserve the democratic label, for it merely engenders demagoguery and mob rule ... Democracy is a political form suitable only to rich, well-structured and highly cultured countries ... In countries where the above conditions are absent ... democracy easily degenerates into ruthless political conflict, because complete freedom of speech and assembly are potent instruments for misguiding the masses.'
ISTVÁN BETHLEN, 1922[7]

war, the chaos resulting from two revolutions and, not least, the economic consequences of Trianon had left the Hungarian economy in ruins and the state on the verge of bankruptcy. Having first brought about Hungary's return to the international community by securing her admission to the League of Nations in 1922, Bethlen deployed in London, Paris and Rome the argument that unless his government could bring inflation under control with the help of foreign loans, Hungary would be unable to pay the reparations imposed upon her at Trianon. His advocacy secured a loan, under League auspices, of 250 million gold crowns which enabled him to eliminate the budgetary deficit by 1924. This, in turn, opened the way for a massive influx of foreign loans and investment which established a basis for full economic recovery. Although agriculture continued to languish for lack of export markets and from competition from cheap American grain, industry revived behind the protective tariff wall which Bethlen erected in 1924; by 1929, industrial output exceeded that of 1913 by 12 per cent and agricultural output by 2 per cent. From 1925 onwards, Bethlen's government was able to post an annual budgetary surplus and consequently substantially to increase investment in education, public health and communications. But this remarkable recovery was dearly bought: by 1931, Hungary had become the most deeply indebted nation in Europe.

In a curious prolongation of the political antagonism between Mihály Károlyi and Bethlen the former, now settled in London where he was popular in left-wing and liberal circles, actively campaigned to undermine Bethlen's efforts to secure loans for Hungary without political strings attached. Károlyi argued that no funds should be made available to Hungary until she had complied fully with every provision of the Trianon Treaty. He made little headway: ... *I tried to make [Ramsay MacDonald] understand the dangers involved in an unconditional loan, but in vain. Labour's attitude in those days was to help the Central Powers, the 'underdog', the victims of Versailles, Trianon and the Imperialists – a mistake bitterly regretted later.*[8] Károlyi's lobbying against the government of his homeland may have influenced that government's decision in 1923 to put him, together with other leading figures in the revolutions of 1918 and 1919, on trial, *in absentia*, for high treason. He was duly found guilty and sentenced, in 1925, to confiscation of all property and permanent exile.

Bethlen's patient and successful pursuit of political and economic stability for Hungary created the preconditions for what had always been his principal goal: the revision of Trianon and recovery of the lost territories. This was not simply the personal aspiration of a statesman who bore the scars of the Hungarian peace delegation's humiliation in Paris; it was an aspiration shared by the overwhelming majority of the Hungarian people and by Hungarian politicians right across the political spectrum, excepting only the outlawed Communists. In order to pursue it, Hungary needed a European ally and some military muscle. Neither Britain nor France could be expected to aid or abet a quest for the revision of the Treaty of which they had been leading architects; and Germany, during the 1920s, gave priority to rebuilding relations with her former enemies. Mussolini's Italy, however, offered a more hopeful prospect; ambitious for the expansion of Italian influence in the Balkans, the Duce shared Hungary's interest in weakening the Little Entente. Bethlen's two meetings with Mussolini in 1927 resulted in the conclusion of a Treaty of Friendship and Co-operation which ended

Hungary's diplomatic isolation – a considerable achievement and largely Bethlen's own. Although lacking in material content beyond a commitment by both sides to resolve any disputes between them peacefully and to hold regular consultations, the Treaty was of considerable importance to Hungary as a demonstration to the rest of Europe that she was no longer friendless. This agreement was to be complemented, in 1930, by a similar treaty between Italy and Austria in 1930; together, the two treaties created the framework for trilateral co-operation, formalised in the Rome Protocols of 1934 creating a customs union between Hungary, Italy and Austria, which gave Hungary a measure of economic and political security. Mussolini also agreed secretly to ship to Hungary a quantity of Austro-Hungarian arms left behind in Italy at the end of the World War. This illegal transaction was subsequently exposed, but Bethlen rode out the resulting storm with little difficulty and resumed his efforts to re-arm Hungary, appointing the extreme right-winger Gyula Gömbös Minister of Defence for the purpose.

However unsavoury his politics, Gömbös proved an effective Minister: by 1932, Hungary had an army of 85,000 men – 50,000 over the limit set by Trianon – including two squadrons equipped with Italian tanks and the rudiments of an air force. Hungary could now hope to be taken more seriously by her neighbours. In 1927, moreover, the revisionist cause was given a boost from an unexpected quarter. Lord Rothermere, the British press baron, dazzled by the charms of the Austrian Princess Stefania Hohenlohe and moved by her laments for dismembered Hungary, launched a campaign in the *Daily Mail* for the revision of Trianon and for the return to Hungary of predominantly Magyar frontier regions.

Rothermere also founded and funded the 'Hungarian

Revisionist League', winning the hysterical gratitude and adulation of the Hungarian public and press – one editorial even urged that he should be offered the Holy Crown. To Bethlen, however, Rothermere's campaigning was not entirely welcome. Not only did it alarm the Little Entente, drawing its members together again just as differing priorities had begun to weaken their network of alliances, but it also promoted what, to Bethlen, was the wrong kind of revision. In a memorandum circulated to his cabinet colleagues in May, 1929, Bethlen laid down that the primary aim of his government's foreign policy was to restore the *integrity* (in the sense of wholeness) of Hungary: those who wished to limit the revisionist movement to ethnic frontiers *forget that this assumption precludes in advance any serious prospect of revision if occasion arises in an unforeseeable political constellation.*[10] This was Bethlen's characteristically opaque way of saying that a bird in the hand was not necessarily worth two in the bush.

LORD ROTHERMERE'S CAMPAIGN FOR THE REVISION OF TRIANON
'Hungary's place in the sun – safety for central europe
Budapest, June 11
... Of the three treaties which rearranged the map of Central Europe, the last and most ill-advised was that of Trianon, which Hungary was called upon to sign on June 4th, 1920. Instead of simplifying the network of nationalities existing there it entangled them still further. So deep is the discontent it has created that every impartial traveler in that part of the Continent sees plainly the need for repairing the mistakes committed. As they now run, the frontiers of the new Central European states are arbitrary and uneconomic. But they have a more serious aspect still. *Their injustice is a standing danger to the peace of Europe ...'*

Extract from Lord Rothermere's leading article in *The Daily Mail* on 21 June 1927[9]

He was not interested in half a loaf. A campaign for revision supported by Italy, perhaps in due course by Germany as well, and backed by a credible threat of military force did not seem, in 1929, an impossible dream.

1929, however, was the year of the financial crash on Wall Street. Its shockwaves engulfed Europe in 1930 and 1931 and no country was harder hit than Hungary. The collapse of agricultural prices and, above all, the sudden calling in of her swollen inventory of short-term loans plunged Hungary into an acute economic crisis which threatened to destroy the recovery so patiently engineered by Bethlen. The deflationary measures which his government now found it necessary to impose provoked widespread public unrest and a wave of strikes which culminated, on 1 September 1930, in a mass demonstration in Budapest in which several hundred marchers and police were injured. Gyula Gömbös, whose success as Minister of Defence had fuelled his ambition to win the premiership, seized the opportunity to discredit Bethlen. He accused the Prime Minister in Horthy's presence of being too lenient towards Hungary's Jewish community whose commanding influence in the Hungarian economy, he argued, was responsible for the country's current problems. Bethlen had, in fact, worked quietly to mitigate the impact of the *Numerus Clausus* law of 1920, which limited Jewish access to higher education. Mindful of the importance of Jewish energy and financial expertise as a key factor in Hungary's economic recovery, he had in 1927 steered through Parliament legislation which significantly diluted the effect of anti-Semitic laws.

Horthy's confidence in Bethlen had already begun to waver. It was further diminished, for the straitlaced Regent, by Bethlen's torrid *affaire* with Countess 'Minci' Széchenyi. The liaison had, in fact, been public knowledge for some time. Bethlen and his wife, Margit, had been living separate lives for several years; Margit, a blue-stocking and would-be romantic novelist, made no secret of her own relationship with Jozsef Görgey, a former officer of the hussars, with whom she frequently appeared in public. Bethlen, for his part, was genuinely in love with Minci Széchenyi and they both took pleasure in long drives in Bethlen's red Lancia roadster. Minci's husband, Count Andor Széchenyi, was fully aware of the relationship and apparently indifferent to it. For Regent Horthy, already disapproving of Bethlen's conduct, the last straw was the discovery that, when the financial crisis reached its nadir in July 1931, his Prime Minister was on holiday with the Countess at the Venice Lido. Bethlen, whose appetite for the cares of office had begun to wane as the economic crisis deepened, decided to jump before he was pushed; on 19 July he tendered his resignation, with that of his cabinet, which Horthy accepted.

Although he remained a powerful and, on the whole, moderating influence in Hungarian politics, Bethlen did not hold office again. For all the musty conservatism of his political beliefs, as Prime Minister he had served Hungary well for a decade. His patient pragmatism had steered his country back from pariah status to full acceptance as a member of the international community. On a political landscape where, during the post-war period, talent was conspicuously lacking István Bethlen was the only man of sufficient stature to represent Hungary effectively on the European stage. He put the lessons learned during his international apprenticeship, at the Paris Peace Conference, to effective use.

10

Károlyi and Bethlen: Endgame

Release from the demands of the premiership enabled Bethlen to concentrate his considerable energies on promoting the cause of revision. In 1932 he accepted the chairmanship of the Revisionist League. He remained a member of Parliament until 1939 and continued to exercise control over the large group of conservative members, including several ministers, who shared his views on foreign policy and his opposition to land reform. He settled easily into the role of *eminence grise* and elder statesman, relishing the exercise of influence without the responsibilities of office. As the years passed and the storm clouds massed around Hungary, Horthy came increasingly to rely on Bethlen's informal advice.

In the preface to a collection of his speeches and writings published in 1933, Bethlen argued that it was impossible to imagine an independent existence or survival for the Hungarian state within the frontiers laid down by Trianon. If Hungary failed to seize the opportunities offered by what might be only a brief respite from armed conflict, the *waves of the sea of Slavs to the north and south and of Romanians will close above our heads*; the Hungarian nation would *sooner or later vanish from the face of the earth.*[1] In this, and in many speeches and articles, Bethlen articulated the deep-seated fear of ethnic extinction and envelopment by Slavdom which had been a recurrent theme in Hungarian history for centuries. In the same year, Bethlen visited the United Kingdom to give a series of lectures, in Cambridge and London, on the implications of Trianon. On the day of his arrival in London, 160 Members of Parliament formed a Parliamentary Committee for the Modification of the Peace of Trianon; and his three lectures were well attended. Bethlen told a London audience: *It is owing to [Trianon] that fully one-third of the Hungarians who had lived for ten centuries in Hungary found themselves outside the new borders of this country and under the domination of Czechs, Rumanians and Serbs ... our national grief and pain on this account is, as you may well imagine, immeasurable. For this very reason, among others, the Hungarian nation never can and never will acquiesce definitely and of its own accord in the Peace Treaty of Trianon.*[2]

Bethlen's maximalist approach to revision did not, however, commend itself to the British Ministers, parliamentarians and Foreign Office officials whom he met during his stay. They were prepared to contemplate support, through the League of Nations, for tinkering with the detail of Trianon in order to iron out some of its more blatant flaws; but they could not countenance the restoration to Hungary of all her lost territories, the re-creation of 'historic Hungary' which Bethlen demanded.

Bethlen's visit to London, and his failure to find backing for his campaign even in that relatively sympathetic capital, had an important impact on his thinking. When his subsequent lobbying of the French, through the French Legation in Budapest, met with an even firmer rebuff, his essential pragmatism took over and, from 1934, he significantly modified his position. Bethlen now began to speak of revision as a long-term goal which could not be attained without the help of a major European ally. In the meantime, Hungary should give priority to monitoring the situation of the Hungarian minorities in the successor states and to campaigning for the protection of their rights. He expressed these views, and his thoughts on other foreign policy issues, in regular articles for the conservative daily *Pesti Napló*.

At about this time, Count Mihály Károlyi's very different views were also undergoing a degree of modification. Since 1925 he had been living in Paris, supported mainly by the fees which he and, more successfully, his wife were able to earn on the lecture circuit. In 1931 he visited the Soviet Union with a group of left-wing writers and, like so many others then and since, was a willing victim of the Soviet propaganda machine. *Nothing I saw*, he subsequently wrote, *however unfavourable, could alter my disposition towards them [the Soviet people]. In the controversy between Trotsky and Stalin about Socialism in one country, I agreed with Stalin, since I cherished no illusions about the strength of the working classes in the West ... As far as human suffering is concerned, was not that inevitably linked up with progress?*[3] Károlyi's views developed on the classic trajectory of those of Western fellow-travellers. During the 1930s, the repeated waves of purges which engulfed Soviet Russia began to erode his faith and he drew back from joining the Communist Party – but it is of interest that he should have even contemplated doing so. In 1939 the Nazi-Soviet Pact deepened his disillusionment; but he remained convinced that, for all its flaws and aberrations in its Soviet context, Communism offered the best hope for mankind.

Meanwhile István Bethlen watched with distaste, but not yet with great disquiet, Hungary's accelerating drift to the right. His successor as Prime Minister, Count Gyula Károlyi, had resigned after only a year in an office whose demands exceeded his modest capabilities. In replacing him, Horthy was mindful of the evident surge in popular support for the radical right and sent for Gyula Gömbös, who also inherited from Bethlen leadership of the Unity Party (which he renamed the 'Party of National Unity'). For a time, Bethlen remained confident that he could keep Gömbös under control. But in 1935, when Gömbös dismissed Bethlen's supporters from the cabinet and then purged them from the Party of National Unity, he realised that he had been mistaken and assumed the leadership of parliamentary opposition to the Gömbös regime. Gömbös made no secret of his ambition to transform Hungary into a fascist, corporate state modelled on and in close alliance with Nazi Germany; during a visit to Germany he also gave Hermann Göring a secret assurance that in Hungary 'the Jewish question' would be resolved. Bethlen was prominent among those who now warned Horthy that Gömbös posed a threat both to the constitution and to the Regent personally. A political crisis was averted only by Gömbös' unexpected death, from kidney disease, in 1936.

Gömbös' departure from the scene did not, however, arrest Hungary's ineluctable drift into the arms of Nazi Germany. A succession of bilateral trade agreements from 1934 onwards tied Hungary's economy ever more closely to that of Germany: by 1939, the Third Reich accounted for over 50 per cent of Hungary's foreign trade. Germany replaced Italy as the strong potential ally which Hungary so badly needed in her quest for the revision of Trianon. In recognition of this, pro-German sentiment steadily increased in most sectors

government's action in this regard is a certificate of poverty for this nation.[6]

Hungarian hopes that a closer relationship with Hitler's Germany, however unequal, might eventually bring its rewards in the shape of a revision of Trianon were not misplaced. The anti-Semitic policies of the Imrédy government, its public – but not material – support for German annexation of the Sudetenland, its agreement to join the Anti-Comintern Pact,* to withdraw from the League of Nations and to conclude a ten-year economic agreement highly favourable to Germany, all combined to impress Hitler sufficiently favourably to result in action on Hungary's behalf (although he never regarded the Hungarians with anything other than contempt). He agreed to mediate, together with Italy, in Hungary's territorial dispute with Czechoslovakia. The outcome, in November 1938, was what became known as the First Vienna Award, under which the Czechoslovak government was bullied by Berlin into returning to Hungary nearly 12,000 square kilometres of Slovakian territory with nearly a million inhabitants, the majority of them ethnic Magyars. Regent Horthy, mounted on his white horse, led a ceremonial procession of the entire Hungarian Parliament – including István Bethlen – into the recovered town of Kassa (Košice). But Bethlen was unimpressed, opposed as ever to settling for half a loaf. He strongly criticised the government for failing to retrieve Pozsony (Bratislava), the ancient seat of the Hungarian Parliament, and that part of Ruthenia (eastern Slovakia) which would have given Hungary a common frontier with Poland.

───────────────

*The agreement concluded in 1936 between Germany and Japan, joined later by Italy, in which each party undertook not to assist the Soviet Union in an attack on the other.

He was less critical of the Second Vienna Award in 1940, again brokered by Germany and Italy, which retrieved for Hungary 43,000 square kilometres of Bethlen's native Transylvania, together with 2.5 million of its inhabitants – nearly half of them Romanian. On 15 September, Bethlen took part in the triumphal entry of Hungarian troops into the Transylvanian town of Kolozsvár (Cluj). He was able to revisit his family estates and to arrange for the renovation of his former home; his satisfaction was nevertheless tinged with apprehension – *I have a dark premonition*, he wrote, *that we shall have to pay dearly for this*.[7]

By this time, however, Bethlen's political career had already come to an end. With the passage through Parliament of the Second Jewish Law in May 1939, further tightening the screw on Hungary's Jewry and imposing disabilities which threatened the livelihood of 250,000 people, a course which in his view invited disaster, Bethlen despaired of being able further to influence the course of Hungarian politics, On the day following the parliamentary vote, he announced his retirement from politics. His farewell letter to his constituents attacked the government's anti-Semitism and its hostility to the landed aristocracy: *Today the only one who is a prophet for the nation is the one who, in the holy name of national interest, eats Jews for breakfast, Counts for lunch and, before going to bed, distributes land and wealth that does not belong to him*.[8]

THE VIENNA AWARDS
The two Vienna Awards, the occupation of Ruthenia in 1939 and, in 1941, of the Hungarian lands awarded to Yugoslavia in 1920, regained for Hungary 78,567 sq.km. of territory – 53 per cent of the losses imposed by the Treaty of Trianon – and 5.3 million people, of whom 42 per cent were ethnic Magyars. Hungary's defeat, as Germany's ally, in 1945 deprived her of all that had been recovered.

Bethlen had never courted popularity and enjoyed it for only a short period in the 1920s before the Depression negated, at least temporarily, the success of his economic policies. His retirement, therefore, was unmourned, even welcomed in many quarters. A few observers, however, were willing to recognise his qualities and his achievement: the Social Democrat daily *Népszava*, for example, declared, from the opposite end of the political spectrum: 'We cannot deny István Bethlen his outstanding talent, his clear insight, the quick recognition of his class interests; we cannot deny that he was the outstanding statesman and politician of post-war Hungary. Few politicians of such great talent remained to the ruling classes of Hungary after the collapse.'[9]

In retirement, which he spent mostly on his country estate in the small village of Inke in western Hungary, Bethlen remained in close touch with his old colleague from Paris days, Pál Teleki, who had succeeded Imrédy as Prime Minister in 1939. Both men agreed, following the outbreak of war in that year, that Hungary's best hope lay in the pursuit of a policy of armed neutrality; and that so far as possible she should keep her distance from Nazi Germany, at the same time strengthening her relations with the Western powers. This was not to be. There was a price to be paid for the two Vienna Awards: the Hungarian government was under pressure not only to resolve 'the Jewish question' to Hitler's satisfaction but also to enter the war in support of his invasion of Russia in June 1941. The pressure on Horthy to comply came not only from Berlin but also from his own General Staff, in which pro-German sentiment predominated: on 27 June, in a decision reinforced by his own hatred of Communism, Horthy sanctioned the advance of 40,000 Hungarian troops into Soviet territory. By the end of the year, Hungary was at war with Great Britain and her Dominions, and also, after Pearl Harbor, with the United States.

Like Horthy, Bethlen believed that the Western democracies would eventually prevail over the Axis powers. Horthy selected him to lead an eventual Hungarian government-in-exile in London in the event of a German occupation of Hungary or the advent to power of the Arrow Cross Party. Both eventualities materialised in 1944 but Bethlen, by that time in poor health, remained in Hungary. He had already made himself thoroughly unpopular in Berlin for criticising the First Vienna Award and now compounded that offence, in German eyes, by speaking out publicly against dictatorships, whether Nazi or Communist.

Characteristically, he attributed their existence to the folly of giving the vote and a secret ballot to the uneducated and easily misled masses. He did not oppose Hungary's dishonourable participation in the invasion of her supposed ally, Yugoslavia, in 1941, despite Pál Teleki's remorseful suicide, with the sole proviso that Hungary should not to acquire Serbian territory beyond that which had been taken from her by Trianon; but he did oppose Hungary's involvement in the German invasion of the Soviet Union, on the grounds that there was no lost territory to be regained there. Following the annihilation of the Hungarian Second Army near Voronezh, on the Eastern Front, in 1942, Bethlen told the Foreign Affairs Committee of

TELEKI'S SUICIDE
In April 1941, only four months after concluding a 'Treaty of Eternal Friendship' with Yugoslavia, Hungary – at Hitler's behest but also in the hope of regaining territory taken from her by Trianon – joined Germany in invading her southern neighbour. Pál Teleki, Prime Minister for the second time, shot himself in remorse, leaving a suicide note addressed to Horthy ending: 'We have taken our stand on the side of scoundrels ... We shall become grave robbers, the most rotten of nations! I did not hold you back. I am guilty. Teleki Pál.' [10]

the Upper House of Parliament: *Had I been asked at the outbreak of war, how will this war end, I would have answered
that the Germans will not win but nor will others. If I were
asked today, I would answer that the Germans have lost the
war but I do not know who will win it.*[11]

Although by 1943 his health had begun rapidly to deterio-
rate, largely as the result of having been a chain-smoker for
most of his adult life – Bethlen agreed to join the Hungarian
National Social Circle, an association of anti-Nazi groups,
and also to become a member of the small informal group
which the Regent had formed to advise him on the conclusion
of a separate peace with the Allies. He supported Horthy's
eventual decision to make a direct approach to Moscow, once
any hope of an Allied invasion of the Balkans had evaporated. In February 1944, he told the Defence Committee of
the Upper House that the war was lost and that Hungary
should seek to conclude a separate peace with the Soviet
Union. When, in March, Horthy was summoned by Hitler
to Schloss Klessheim in Austria to be berated for Hungary's
contacts with the Allies, of which the Germans had been
aware from the beginning, and told of Hitler's decision to
occupy Hungary in consequence, Bethlen, fearing kidnap,
strongly advised the Regent not to go. Horthy went nevertheless, returning on 19 March effectively under Nazi escort, as
eight German divisions poured across the Hungarian frontier
to occupy the territory of their notional ally.

Gestapo units immediately began to round up and arrest
known opponents of the government and other 'undesirables'.
Finding Bethlen closeted with the Prime Minister, Miklós
Kállay, in the latter's office, two Gestapo officers asked him
to accompany them to the German Embassy; Bethlen refused
and, heavily disguised and carrying false papers, succeeded in

escaping to western Hungary where he went into hiding. There followed a game of cat and mouse in which Bethlen found refuge in the houses of a succession of friends and supporters, in both Hungary and Transylvania. The Gestapo failed to find him. He continued to maintain direct contact with the Regent, even risking visits to Budapest in July and August, at Horthy's request, to discuss the formation of a new government under General Lakatos-Kállay, whom the Germans detested, had been obliged to seek asylum in the Turkish Legation. During further meetings in September, Bethlen strengthened Horthy's resolve to open secret negotiations with the Russians for an armistice. A preliminary armistice was duly signed, in Moscow and without the knowledge of a Hungarian cabinet which contained pro-Nazi ministers, on 11 October.

By mid-December 1944, the advancing Red Army had swept across the Great Hungarian Plain and broken the German line east of Budapest; by Christmas, the capital had been surrounded and a siege begun which was to last for nearly two months. Other Soviet forces by-passed Budapest and advanced into western Hungary, where Bethlen was once more in hiding near Lake Balaton. The stress and anxieties of the previous months had taken their toll: he was now suffering from a duodenal ulcer and had had two minor heart attacks. Partly in order to secure medical attention and partly to avoid putting the lives of his temporary hosts at risk, Bethlen gave himself up to the local Soviet commander. Aware of his political importance but less so of his political views, the Russians held him under house arrest but treated him well. By February 1945, the Russians had done their homework and identified Bethlen as an arch-conservative reactionary who should have no place in Hungary's political future. He was flown to Moscow in March and held in the hospital of the notorious

Butyrka prison, where his health rapidly deteriorated. From Hungary, Bethlen's wife Margit petitioned Stalin for her husband's release or, at least, for permission to correspond with him; she received no reply. The new centre-left Hungarian government declined to lend its support, preferring to keep Bethlen out of Hungary's post-war politics.

István Bethlen died in the Butyrka on 5 October 1946, after a massive heart attack. He was buried in a common grave in the cemetery of the Donskoi Monastery. His remains were never recovered. In 1994 his symbolic ashes were interred in Budapest's Kerepesi Cemetery, close to the graves and monuments of other Hungarian statesmen.

Mihály Károlyi, meanwhile, had spent the war in England, living first in North Oxford and then in Hampstead. He founded the New Democratic Hungary movement, of which branches were established throughout the Hungarian diaspora; and continued to promote his vision of a post-war Danube Federation. He maintained close relations with the Soviet Embassy and with the Ambassador, Ivan Maisky, personally. With Maisky's help, Károlyi made contact with the Hungarian Communist Mátyás Rákosi in Moscow and tried to interest the future Hungarian dictator in a project for the formation of a Hungarian Legion from Hungarians in Soviet prisoner-of-war camps. He received no response. His war effort was limited to broadcasting messages of encouragement to the Hungarian people on the BBC's Hungarian service.

Following the elections of November 1945 – the most free and democratic ever held in Hungary – Károlyi was repeatedly invited by the Social Democratic Party, now in close alliance with the Communists, to return to Hungary and to take on a political role. Hints were dropped that he would be a strong candidate for the Presidency of the Republic. When, in

March 1946, the National Assembly had repealed the law of 1925 confiscating his property, Károlyi returned to his home-land after an absence of 27 years. He was received with great ceremony by the Prime Minister, Ferenc Nagy (leader of the Smallholders' Party), and official receptions were held in his honour. Popular reaction to his return was, however, muted. In an ironic turn of the historical wheel, he accepted an invita-tion to join the Hungarian delegation to the 1946 Paris Peace Conference and spoke there in support of Hungary's unsuc-cessful plea to be allowed to retain the territory returned to her by the two Vienna Awards. The Czechoslovak leader, Jan Masaryk, remarked that Károlyi's speech could have been delivered by István Bethlen. In 1947, as the Communists tightened their grip on Hungary, Károlyi was appointed to represent his country as Minister in Paris, accredited simulta-neously to the Netherlands, Belgium and Luxembourg.

As Rákosi's reign of terror engulfed Hungary after the seizure of total power by the Communist Party in 1948, Károlyi became increasingly – and belatedly – disillusioned. Senior members of his staff in the Hungarian Legation were recalled to Budapest and disappeared. When the Catholic Primate of Hungary, Cardinal Mindszenty, was arrested in December 1948, Károlyi attempted to intercede on his behalf; and, following the Cardinal's trial in February 1949, urged that his sentence to life imprisonment should be commuted to exile. When his appeals were ignored, Károlyi resigned his post and voluntarily returned to a life of exile. He lived with his wife in the village of Vence, in the Mediterranean Alps, where he wrote his disappointingly uninformative memoirs; and where he died in 1955, not living to witness the brave uprising of his countrymen against Communist dictatorship and Russian occupation a year later.

Epilogue

Hungary has sustained, and survived, a number of disasters in her thousand-year history, among them the Mongol invasions of the 13th century, defeat by the Ottoman Turks at Mohács in 1526, the crushing by Austria and Russia of her bid for independence in 1849, defeat in two World Wars, Mátyás Rákosi's reign of terror in the 1950s and the bloody suppression by Soviet tanks of the 1956 uprising. The Treaty of Trianon eclipsed all of these in severity because its consequences were permanent. The wounds inflicted by invasion, defeat and repression may be deep but they heal. Amputation is irreversible.

The terms imposed upon Hungary by the Paris Peace Conference were not, in the main, the product of malice, revenge nor even of any powerful urge to punish. They resulted partly from the faulty structure of the Conference itself and partly from a fatigue-induced disinclination to take a second look at a complex web of demographic and territorial issues; but mainly from the determination of the Allies to satisfy and consecrate the national aspirations of the formerly subject peoples of the Austro-Hungarian Monarchy. Hungary, like Austria, was by 1919 reconciled to the loss of the 'nationalities' and to that of some of the territory on which they lived. Hungary could not, however, reconcile herself to the loss of three million ethnic Magyars, condemned by Trianon to live under alien rule. The bitterness engendered by this avoidable injustice poisoned Hungarian politics between the two World Wars and fed the dark side of the Hungarian national psyche.

It is possible that, even had the terms of peace imposed on her in 1920 been less punitive, Hungary would still have drawn close to Nazi Germany. Pro-German sentiment had always been strong in Hungary and, after the Kun inoculation, it was natural that her rulers in the 1930s should gravitate towards the strongest enemy of Soviet Communism. It is unlikely, however, that Hungary would willingly have become Hitler's ally in the Second World War if the nation had not been obsessed with the quest for revision and, as a result, lured into a Faustian pact which held out the prospect of recovering the lost territories. István Bethlen's instinct, which Horthy and most Hungarian politicians shared, was to maintain good relations with Germany but to keep their distance; when war broke out in 1939, armed neutrality was their preference. But by then, with the first Vienna Award, Hungary had already put herself in debt to Hitler and had taken the first fatal step down the slippery slope which led to wartime alliance, military disaster on the Russian front, the mass murder of Hungary's Jewish community and occupation first by Germany and then, for 45 years, by the Soviet Union.

Most of the three million Magyars who, after 1920, had to live their lives outside their homeland and educate their children to a different allegiance found that they could hope for no more than second-class status in the national societies of which they had become involuntary members. This was particularly the case in Transylvania, where the Magyar population suffered serious civil disabilities, especially in higher education, both before and during the period of Romanian Communist rule. Concern for their situation, and competition to be seen as their most effective champions, became and, after an interval during most of the Communist period, remains a sensitive issue in the domestic politics of Hungary.

In 2001 a centre-right Hungarian government introduced a Status Law which, on paper, conferred a number of social and financial benefits on ethnic Magyars living in Slovakia, Romania, Ukraine, former Yugoslavia and Slovenia; the socialist opposition felt unable to oppose the measure, which was carried in the Hungarian Parliament by 306 votes to 17. Inevitably, the law generated friction between Hungary and her neighbours and, even when modified in 2003, proved difficult or impossible to implement. But after the eventual accession of Serbia, all Hungary's neighbours except Ukraine will be, like her, members of the European Union: this should reduce the significance, and the damaging impact, of the frontiers drawn up by the Paris Peace Conference in 1919. The history of East-Central Europe during the past 90 years nevertheless provides a graphic demonstration of the extent to which the consequences of bias, errors and misjudgements on the part of statesmen, diplomats and their advisors can far outlive their perpetrators.

> 'Trianon to us bears the meaning of a human slaughterhouse: it is there that every third Hungarian was crushed into subsistence under foreign rule; it is there that the territories of our native language were torn to pieces.'
>
> GYULA ILLYÉS, HUNGARY'S LEADING MODERN POET, WRITING IN 1980[1]

Notes

Prologue

1. *The Times*, 9 June 1896.

1: Hungary's Thousand Years

1. P Body (ed.), *Hungarian Statesmen of Destiny, 1860–1960* (Boulder, Col.: 1989) p 89.
2. N Stone, 'Hungary and the Crisis of 1914', *Journal of Contemporary History*, Vol. I, (1966) p 168.
3. J Galántai, *Hungary in the First World War* (Budapest: 1989) p 18.

2: Mihály Károlyi and István Bethlen

1. I Romsics, *István Bethlen: A Great Conservative Statesman of Hungary, 1874–1946* (New York: 1995) p 54, hereafter Romsics, *Bethlen*.
2. Romsics, *Bethlen*, p 45.
3. H Seton-Watson & C Seton-Watson, *The Making of a New Europe: R.W. Seton-Watson and the Last Years of Austria-Hungary* (London: 1981) p 201.
4. Galántai, *Hungary in the First World War*, p 231.

5. Galántai, *Hungary in the First World War*, p 234.
6. G Vermes, *István Tisza* (New York: 1985) p 382.

3: Collapse and Revolution

1. Count M Károlyi, *Faith without Illusion: the Memoirs of Michael Károlyi* (London: 1956) p 102.
2. G Vermes, 'István Tisza', in Pál Bődy (ed), *Hungarian Statesmen of Destiny, 1860–1960* (New York: 1989) p 95.
3. Károlyi, *Faith without Illusion*, p 123.
4. G Vermes, 'The October Revolution in Hungary: from Károlyi to Kun', in I Völgyes (ed), *Hungary in Revolution, 1918–1919: Nine Essays* (Lincoln, Nebraska: 1971) p 41.
5. P Pastor, *Hungary Between Wilson and Lenin: The Hungarian Revolution of 1918–1919 and the Big Three* (Boulder, Colorado and New York: 1976) p 90.
6. W Beveridge, *Power and Influence* (London: 1953) pp 155–6.
7. Károlyi, *Faith without Illusion*, p 150.
8. J Bátki (ed), *Krúdy's Chronicles* (Budapest: 2000) p 245.

4: Prelude to Paris

1. Galántai, *Hungary in the First World War*, p 274.
2. D Lloyd George, *War Memoirs* (London: 1938) Vol. II, p 1480.
3. I Romsics, *The Dismantling of Historic Hungary: The Peace Treaty of Trianon, 1920* (New York: 2002) p 36.
4. H Seton-Watson, 'R.W. Seton-Watson and the Trianon Settlement', in B K Király, P Pastor & I Sanders (eds), *Essays on World War I: Total War and Peacemaking – A Case Study on Trianon* (New York: 1982) p 46.

5. M Lojkó, *British Policy on Hungary, 1918–1919: A Documentary Sourcebook* (London: 1995) p 4.
6. C A Macartney & A W Palmer, *Independent Eastern Europe* (London: 1967) p 84.
7. Seton-Watson & Seton-Watson, *The Making of a New Europe*, p 292.

5: Károlyi Abdicates

1. E Ashmead-Bartlett, *The Tragedy of Central Europe* (London: 1923) p 76.
2. S Bonsal, *Unfinished Business* (London: 1944) p 119.
3. H Nicolson, *Peacemaking 1919* (London: 1933) p 298.
4. W K Hancock & J Van der Poel (eds), *Selection from the Smuts Papers* (Cambridge: 1966) Vol. IV, p 86.
5. H N Brailsford, *Across the Blockade* (London: 1919) p 14.
6. Quoted in A C János, *The Politics of Backwardness in Hungary, 1825–1945* (Princeton: 1982) p 194.

6: Dismemberment

1. Nicholson, *Peacemaking*, p 34.
2. Nicholson, *Peacemaking*, p 126.
3. Nicholson, *Peacemaking*, p 127.
4. Nicholson, *Peacemaking*, pp 100 and 122–3.
5. Nicholson, *Peacemaking*, p 275.
6. D Lloyd George, *The Truth About the Peace Treaties* (London: 1938) Vol. II, p 920.
7. Lloyd George, *The Truth About the Peace Treaties*, Vol. I, p 406.
8. F Deák, *Hungary at the Paris Peace Conference* (New York: 1942) p 444.

9. M Bánffy, *The Phoenix Land* (Budapest: 1932, and London (trans.): 2003) p 240.

10. Deák, *Hungary at the Paris Peace Conference*, p 105.

11. R Tökes, *Béla Kun and the Hungarian Soviet Republic* (New York: 1967) pp 203–4.

7: Counter-revolution

1. In Ashmead-Bartlett, *The Tragedy of Central Europe*.

2. Ashmead-Bartlett, *The Tragedy of Central Europe*, p 191.

3. Deák, *Hungary at the Paris Peace Conference*, p 115.

4. Deák, *Hungary at the Paris Peace Conference*, p 120.

5. Deák, *Hungary at the Paris Peace Conference*, pp 135–6.

6. Maj. Gen. H H Bandholtz, *An Undiplomatic Diary* (New York: 1933; reprinted 1966) p 127.

7. Bandholtz, *An Undiplomatic Diary*, pp 151–4.

8. Bandholtz, *An Undiplomatic Diary*, pp 184–5.

9. I Romsics, *Hungary in the Twentieth Century* (Budapest: 1999) p 111.

10. Gy Juhász, *Hungarian Foreign Policy, 1919–1945* (Budapest: 1979) p 34.

8: Paris

1. Count A Apponyi, *The Memoirs of Count Apponyi* (London: 1935) p 253.

2. Apponyi, *The Memoirs of Count Apponyi*, p 266.

3. Romsics, *The Dismantling of Historic Hungary*, pp 126–7.

4. Quoted from contemporary press reports in Romsics, *The Dismantling of Historic Hungary*, pp 128–9.

5. Parliamentary Debates: Official Report, 5th Series, House of Commons, Vol. 125, column 272.

6. Parliamentary Debates: Official Report, 5th Series, House of Lords, Vol. XXXIX, column 148.

7. Parliamentary Debates: Official Report, 5th Series, House of Lords, Vol. XXXIX, columns 786–787.

8. Documents on British Foreign Policy, 1919–1939, First Series, Vol. VII, p 248.

9. Documents on British Foreign Policy, 1919–1939, First Series, Vol. VII, p 386.

10. Documents on British Foreign Policy, 1919–1939, First Series, Vol. VII, pp 440–4.

11. Romsics, *The Dismantling of Historic Hungary*, p 137.

12. Romsics, *The Dismantling of Historic Hungary*, p 144.

13. Romsics, *The Dismantling of Historic Hungary*, p 145

14. Deák, *Hungary at the Paris Peace Conference*, pp 551–4.

15. Romsics, *The Dismantling of Historic Hungary*, p 147.

9: Bethlen – Consolidation and Recovery

1. Romsics, *The Dismantling of Historic Hungary*, p 152.

2. Romsics, *The Dismantling of Historic Hungary*, p 152.

3. Romsics, *The Dismantling of Historic Hungary*, p 153.

4. Deák, *Hungary at the Paris Peace Conference*, p 550.

5. For a full account of these two misguided adventures, see B Cartledge, *The Will to Survive: A History of Hungary* (London: 2005) pp 351–3.

6. Bánffy, *The Phoenix Land*, p 240.

7. János, *The Politics of Backwardness in Hungary*, p 210.

8. Károlyi, *Faith without Illusion*, p 205.

9. Viscount Rothermere, *My Campaign for Hungary* (London: 1939) p 60.

10. Juhász, *Hungarian Foreign Policy*, p 86.

10: Károlyi and Bethlen: Endgame

1. Romsics, *Bethlen*, p 306.
2. Count S Bethlen, *The Treaty of Trianon and European Peace: Four Lectures Delivered in London in 1933* (London: 1934) p 65.
3. Károlyi, *Faith without Illusion*, p 251.
4. T Sakmyster, *Hungary's Admiral on Horseback: Miklós Horthy, 1918–1944* (Boulder, Colorado: 1994) p 206.
5. I Mócsy, 'Count István Bethlen', in Bődy (ed), *Hungarian Statesmen of Destiny*, p 147.
6. Romsics, *Bethlen*, p 343.
7. Romsics, *Bethlen*, p 357.
8. Romsics, *Bethlen*, p 351.
9. Romsics, *Bethlen*, p 351.
10. There are several versions of the text of Teleki's suicide note. The excerpt given here is my translation from the facsimile of the original manuscript, reproduced in M Szinai & L Szücs, *The Confidential Papers of Admiral Horthy* (Budapest: 1965) between pp 178 and 179.
11. Romsics, *Bethlen*, p 366.

Epilogue

1. Gy Illyés, 'Íroi gondok' ['A Writer's Concerns'] in *Tiszataj*, September 1980.

Chronology

YEAR	AGES (BETHLEN/ KÁROLYI)	TWO LIVES AND THE LAND
1874		István Bethlen is born in Transylvania.
1875		Mihályi Károlyi is born in Fót, near Budapest.
1901	27/26	Bethlen is elected to Parliament and marries.
1910	36/35	Károlyi is elected to Parliament.
1912	38/37	Károlyi fights a duel with Prime Minister Tisza.
1914	40/39	Károlyi marries Catherine Andrássy and, like Bethlen, volunteers for military service.
1916	42/41	Emperor Franz Josef dies, aged 86. Károlyi forms a new political party, opposed to the war.

YEAR	HISTORY	CULTURE
1874	End of Ashanti War. Britain annexes Fiji Islands.	Thomas Hardy, *Far from the Madding Crowd*.
1875	Britain buys Suez Canal shares from Khedive of Egypt.	Mark Twain, *The Adventures of Tom Sawyer*.
1901	Death of Queen Victoria.	Rudyard Kipling, *Kim*.
1910	Liberals win British General Election.	H G Wells, *The History of Mr. Polly*.
1912	*Titanic* sinks. First Balkan War	C G Jung, *The Theory of Psychoanalysis*.
1914	Outbreak of First World War: Battles of Mons, the Marne and First Ypres. Russians defeated at Battles of Tannenberg and Masurian Lakes.	James Joyce, *Dubliners*. Film: Charlie Chaplin in *Making a Living*.
1916	First World War. Battles of Verdun and the Somme. US President Woodrow Wilson is re-elected and issues Peace Note to belligerents in European war.	James Joyce, *Portrait of an Artist as a Young Man*. Film: *Intolerance*.

YEAR	AGES (BETHLEN/ KÁROLYI)	TWO LIVES AND THE LAND
1918	44/43	Oct: Austro-Hungarian Monarchy falls apart. Tisza acknowledges that war is lost; he is murdered two weeks later. Károlyi forms National Council, which seizes power in the 'Aster Revolution'. Károlyi appointed Prime Minister.
		Nov: Parliament abolishes Monarchy and proclaims the Hungarian republic. Károlyi negotiates an armistice with the Allies. Czech, Romanian and Serbian troops invade and occupy large areas of Hungary. Béla Kun returns to Hungary from Russia.
1919	45/44	Jan: Károlyi assumes Presidency of Hungary. The Peace Conference opens in Paris.
		Feb: Bethlen forms counter-revolutionary Party of National Unity.
		Mar: Károlyi inaugurates land reform. Béla Kun and the Communists take over. Bethlen escapes to Vienna.
		Apr: Smuts visits Budapest on behalf of the Peace Conference. Romanian troops advance further into Hungary. In Vienna, Bethlen becomes head of the Anti-Bolshevik Committee.
		May: Kun's 'Red Army' defeats the Romanians and drives the Czechs out of Hungary. Bethlen's colleagues burgle the Hungarian Legation in Vienna.
		Jun: The Council of Four publishes proposals for Hungary's future frontiers and orders a cessation of hostilities.
		Jul/Aug: 'Red Army' withdraws from Slovakia; new offensive against Romanians fails. Kun's regime collapses. Károlyi leaves for exile in Prague.
		Aug: Romanians occupy Budapest. Bethlen returns from Vienna.

YEAR	HISTORY	CULTURE
1918	First World War.	Gerald Manley Hopkins, *Poems.*
	Peace Treaty of Brest-Litovsk between Russia and the Central Powers.	Luigi Pirandello, *Six Characters in Search of an Author.*
	German Spring offensives on Western Front fail.	
	Allied offensives on Western Front have German army in full retreat.	
	Armistice signed between Allies and Germany.	
1919	Communist Revolt in Berlin.	Bauhaus movement founded by Walter Gropius.
	Paris Peace Conference adopts principle of founding League of Nations.	Paul Klee, *Dream Birds.*
	Benito Mussolini founds fascist movement in Italy.	Thomas Hardy, *Collected Poems.*
	Treaty of Versailles signed.	Herman Hesse, *Demian.*
	British-Persian agreement at Tehran to preserve integrity of Persia.	George Bernard Shaw, *Heartbreak House.*
	Irish War of Independence begins.	*Three-Cornered Hat.*
	US Senate votes against ratification of Versailles Treaty, leaving the USA outside the League of Nations.	Film: *The Cabinet of Dr Caligari.*

YEAR	AGES (BETHLEN/ KÁROLYI)	TWO LIVES AND THE LAND
1919 (cont.)		Sep: The Council of Four sends Sir George Clerk to Bucharest to remonstrate over Romanian conduct. Admiral Horthy's National Army unleashes 'White Terror' in western Hungary.
		Oct: Clerk brokers the formation of a coalition government which Peace Conference can recognise.
		Nov: Romanians withdraw from Budapest. Admiral Horthy leads the National Army into the capital.
		Dec: Hungary invited to send delegation to the Paris Peace Conference.
1920	46/45	Jan: Count Albert Apponyi is given the draft peace treaty in Paris and presents Hungary's case against it to the Peace Conference.
		Feb: The Hungarian delegation presents a detailed critique of the draft treaty to the Peace Conference.
		Mar: Lloyd George expresses misgivings over the severity of the terms offered to Hungary. Admiral Horthy is elected Regent of Hungary.
		May: The Allies inform Hungary in writing that the terms of peace originally drawn up must stand without modification.
		Jun: The Treaty of Trianon is signed.
1921	47/46	István Bethlen becomes Prime Minister, inaugurates Hungary's economic recovery and presides over the campaign for the revision of the Treaty of Trianon.

YEAR	HISTORY	CULTURE
1920	League of Nations comes into existence.	F Scott Fitzgerald, *This Side of Paradise*.
	The Hague is selected as seat of International Court of Justice.	Franz Kafka, *The Country Doctor*.
	League of Nations headquarters moved to Geneva.	Rambert School of Ballet formed.
	Warren G Harding wins US Presidential election.	
	Bolsheviks win Russian Civil War.	
	Government of Ireland Act passed.	
	Adolf Hitler announces his 25-point programme in Munich.	
1921	Paris Conference of wartime allies fixes Germany's reparation payments.	D H Lawrence, *Women in Love*.
	Irish Free State established.	
	Washington Naval Treaty signed.	

YEAR	AGES (BETHLEN/ KÁROLYI)	TWO LIVES AND THE LAND
1922	48/47	Hungary is admitted to the League of Nations.
1923	49/48	The Hungarian government tries Károlyi, *in absentia,* for high treason.
1925	51/50	Károlyi is sentenced to loss of all property and to permanent exile.
1927	53/52	Bethlen negotiates a Treaty of Friendship and Co-operation with Italy.
1930	56/55	Hungary is plunged into economic crisis by the Wall Street Crash.
1931	57/56	Bethlen resigns the premiership. Károlyi visits the Soviet Union.
1932	58/57	Bethlen becomes Chairman of the Revisionist League.
1938	64/63	Following the *Anschluss*, Bethlen warns Parliament against too close alignment with Nazi Germany and opposes anti-Jewish legislation. The First Vienna Award restores to Hungary a large area of Slovakia.

YEAR	HISTORY	CULTURE
1922	League of Nations council approves British mandate in Palestine.	T S Eliot, *The Waste Land.*
1923	French and Belgian troops occupy the Ruhr.	P G Wodehouse, *The Inimitable Jeeves.*
	Adolf Hitler's *coup d'état* (The Beer Hall Putsch) fails.	BBC listings magazine *Radio Times* first published.
1925	Hitler reorganises Nazi Party.	Noel Coward, *Hay Fever.*
	Locarno Treaty signed in London.	Film: *Battleship Potemkin.*
1927	Inter-Allied military control of Germany ends.	Virginia Woolf, *To the Lighthouse.*
	'Black Friday' in Germany – the economic system collapses.	Film: *The Jazz Singer.*
1930	London Naval Treaty signed.	W H Auden, *Poems.*
	Nazi party in Germany gains 107 seats.	Film: *All Quiet on the Western Front.*
1931	National Government formed in Great Britain.	Films: *Dracula. Little Caesar.*
1932	F D Roosevelt wins US Presidential election in Democrat landslide.	Aldous Huxley, *Brave New World.*
1938	Munich Agreement hands Sudetenland to Germany.	Graham Greene, *Brighton Rock.*
	Kristallnacht in Germany – Jewish houses, synagogues and schools burn for a week.	Ballpoint pen patented in Hungary.
		Film:. *The Adventures of Robin Hood.*

YEAR	AGES (BETHLEN/ KÁROLYI)	TWO LIVES AND THE LAND
1939	65/64	Bethlen retires from political life.
1940	66/65	Hungary and Romania join Axis. Under the Second Vienna Award, Hungary regains a large area of Transylvania which includes Bethlen's family estates.
1941	67/66	Hungary joins Germany in the invasion of her ally, Yugoslavia. Prime Minister Teleki shoots himself.
1943	69/68	The Hungarian Second Army is annihilated on the Eastern Front, near Voronezh.
1944	70/69	Germany invades and occupies Hungary. Bethlen goes into hiding. The siege of Budapest begins in December.

YEAR	HISTORY	CULTURE
1939	Germans troops enter Prague. German invasion of Poland: Britain and France declare war. Soviets invade Finland.	John Steinbeck, *The Grapes of Wrath*. Film: *Gone with the Wind*.
1940	Second World War: Churchill becomes Prime Minister. Germany invades France. Italy declares war on France and Britain. Italy invades Greece.	Ernest Hemingway, *For Whom the Bell Tolls*. Films: *Pinocchio. Rebecca*.
1941	Second World War. Germany invades USSR Japan attacks Pearl Harbor.	Noel Coward, *Blithe Spirit*. Films: *Citizen Kane. Dumbo. The Maltese Falcon*.
1943	Second World War. Germans surrender at Stalingrad. Invasion of Sicily and Italy. Tehran Conference: Churchill, Roosevelt and Stalin meet.	Rogers and Hammerstein, *Oklahoma!* Film: *For Whom the Bell Tolls. Bataan*.
1944	D-Day landings in France. British and US forces in Italy liberate Rome. German counter-offensive in the Ardennes.	Terrence Rattigan, *The Winslow Boy*. Film: *Double Indemnity. Henry V. Meet Me in St Louis*.

YEAR	AGES (BETHLEN/ KÁROLYI)	TWO LIVES AND THE LAND
1945	71/70	Bethlen gives himself up to the Russians and is flown to Moscow.
1946	72/71	Bethlen dies in the Butyrka prison hospital, Moscow, on 5 October. Károlyi returns to a ceremonial welcome in Hungary after 27 years of exile and joins the Hungarian delegation to the second Paris Peace Conference.
1947	73/72	Károlyi is appointed Minister in Paris
1949	–/74	Károlyi resigns his post and returns to exile, in France.
1955	–/80	Károlyi dies on 19 March.

YEAR	HISTORY	CULTURE
1945	Second World War. Hitler commits suicide in Berlin, and the city surrenders to Soviets. VE Day: 8 May. USA drops atomic bombs on Hiroshima and Nagasaki. Japan surrenders to Allies.	George Orwell, *Animal Farm*. Evelyn Waugh, *Brideshead Revisited*. Films: *Brief Encounter. The Way to the Stars*.
1946	UN General Assembly opens in London. Churchill's 'Iron Curtain' speech. Nuremberg establishes guilty verdicts for war crimes.	Bertrand Russell, *History of Western Philosophy.*. Film: *Great Expectations*. Radio: Alistair Cook's *Letter from America* begins (series ends in 2004).
1947	'Truman Doctrine' pledges to support 'free peoples resisting subjugation by armed minorities or outside pressures'. Indian Independence and Partition.	Tennessee Williams, *A Streetcar Named Desire*. Films: *Monsieur Verdoux. Black Narcissus*.
1949	Foundation of North Atlantic Treaty Organisation (NATO). Berlin blockade is lifted. USSR tests its first atomic bomb.	George Orwell, *Nineteen Eighty-Four*. Arthur Miller, *Death of a Salesman*. Film: *The Third Man*.
1955	USSR declares end of war with Germany. Churchill resigns as Prime Minister: replaced by Anthony Eden.	Vladimir Nabokov, *Lolita*. Film: *The Seven Year Itch*.

YEAR	AGES (BETHLEN/ KÁROLYI)	TWO LIVES AND THE LAND
1962		Károlyi's remains are returned to Hungary and given a state funeral.
1994		Bethlen's symbolic remains are given a ceremonial burial in Budapest.

YEAR	HISTORY	CULTURE
1962	Cuban Missile Crisis.	Alexander Solzhenitsyn, *One day in the Life of Ivan Denisovich.* Film: *Dr No.*
1994	Nelson Mandela sworn in as president of South Africa. Russian forces invade Chechnya.	Eric Hobsbawm, *Age of Extremes, The Short Twentieth Century.* Film: *The Madness of King George.*

Further Reading

There is no biography of Mihály Károlyi in English, so the English reader is dependent on his memoirs, *Faith Without Illusion* (London: 1956), and on those of his wife, *A Life Together* (London: 1966). As both books were written so long after the events they describe they are short on detail but give a good and atmospheric picture of Hungary before and during the First World War. The only substantial biography of Károlyi is in Hungarian: *Károlyi Mihály: politikai életrajz (Mihály Károlyi: a political biography)* by Tibor Hajdu (Budapest: 1978). István Bethlen has fared better. *István Bethlen: A Great Conservative Statesman of Hungary, 1874–1946* (New York: 1995) by Ignác Romsics is an excellent and detailed biography, less uncritical than its title might suggest, and well translated from Hungarian by Mario Fenyo. There is also a useful biographical sketch, 'Count István Bethlen' by István Mócsy in *Hungarian Statesmen of Destiny, 1860–1960* (New York: 1989), edited by Pál Bődy.

Both Károlyi and Bethlen naturally feature prominently in general histories of Hungary, of which the most recent is my *The Will to Survive: A History of Hungary* (London: 2005), also published in Hungarian as *Megmaradni* (Budapest:

2008). *The Hungarians* by Paul Lendvai (London: 2003) is a very readable and entertaining account with a biographical approach by a Hungarian journalist who left his country in 1956 and became a distinguished correspondent on the *Financial Times*. Miklós Molnár's *Concise History of Hungary* (Cambridge: 2001) is shorter and has more of a textbook structure; but it is reliable and well-illustrated. *A History of Hungary: Millennium in Central Europe,* by László Kontler (London: 2002), written in English by a Hungarian academic, has a more philosophical approach and is based on the author's lectures to non-Hungarian students in the Central European University. The best history of 20th-century Hungary in English is by Ignác Romsics: *Hungary in the Twentieth Century* (Budapest: 1999).

Among more specialised accounts, pride of place must go to C A Macartney's monumental *October Fifteenth: A History of Modern Hungary, 1929–1945* (Edinburgh: 1957), in two volumes, which recounts the political events leading up to, and during, the Second World War not just day by day but almost minute by minute; it benefits not only from the author's encyclopaedic knowledge of all things Hungarian but also from the fact that he was personally acquainted with many of Hungary's leading politicians between the wars, including István Bethlen. *The Phoenix Land* by Miklós Bánffy (London: 2003) is a hugely entertaining political memoir by a Transylvanian aristocrat who served briefly as Hungary's Foreign Minister in the 1920s, covering the interwar and wartime periods. The same writer's fictional but factually based *Transylvanian Trilogy* (London: 1999–2001), translated by Patrick Thursfield and Katalin Bánffy-Jelen, is an unforgettable portrait of pre-1914 Hungary and the ideal introduction for readers unfamiliar with that country. The best account of Béla Kun's 133-day Communist regime is that by Rudolf Tökés in *Béla Kun and the Hungarian Soviet Republic* (New York: 1967), while *Bolshevism in Hungary: the Béla Kun Period*, by Albert Kaas and Fedor de Lazarovics (London: 1931) contains important documentary material. The best biography of Miklós Horthy is by Thomas Sakmyster, *Hungary's Admiral on Horseback: Miklós Horthy 1918–1944* (Boulder, Colorado: 1994), which also conveys a clear picture of Hungarian politics and society between the wars. An essential complement to it is *Honour and Duty* (Lewes: 2005) by Horthy's daughter-in-law, Countess Ilona Edelsheim Gyulai, which gives a fascinating first-hand account of life in the Regent's family during the Second World War. Miklós Horthy also wrote his memoirs – *Memoirs* (New York: 1957) – but they are stilted and not very informative. Tibor Frank has edited and introduced the papers of J F Montgomery, US Minister to Hungary from 1933 to 1941, in *Discussing Hitler* (Budapest and New York: 2003), which provides invaluable insights into Hungarian politics between the wars.

Turning to books more directly concerned with the events described in the present volume, Peter Pastor's *Hungary Between Wilson and Lenin: The Hungarian Revolution of 1918–1919* (New York: 1976) and *Hungary in Revolution, 1918–19* edited by István Völgyes (Lincoln, Nebraska: 1971) both give good accounts of the Károlyi revolution. Maj. Gen. Harry Bandholtz, the American leader of the Inter-Allied Military Mission to Hungary in 1919–20, kept a detailed and entertaining diary, large extracts of which were re-published in 1966 as *An Undiplomatic Diary* (New York: 1966); they give a vivid picture of life in Hungary during the Romanian occupation.

On the Paris Peace Conference itself and Hungary's belated

involvement in it, the most comprehensive (although it is a short book) and reliable account is in *The Dismantling of Historic Hungary: the Peace Treaty of Trianon, 1920* by Ignác Romsics (New York: 2002). Margaret Macmillan's superb *Peacemakers: Six Months That Changed the World* (London: 2001) contains a short chapter on Hungary but considerations of space naturally precluded a fuller treatment. The fullest, but not always the most reliable, treatment of the evolution of the Treaty of Trianon is Ferenc Deák's *Hungary at the Paris Peace Conference: the Diplomatic History of the Treaty of Trianon* (New York: 1942). *The Making of a New Europe: R. W. Seton-Watson and the Last Years of Austria-Hungary* by Hugh and Christopher Seton-Watson (London: 1981) is indispensable for the insights it provides into the thinking and priorities of the Allies in the years leading up to the Peace Conference and into the influences which shaped them. Perhaps the most valuable source of all, not only for the Austro-Hungarian dimension of the Conference but for all its workings, is Harold Nicolson's *Peacemaking 1919* (London: 1933), a classic in its own right. A similar, less colourful but equally useful account, giving the American perspective, is *At the Paris Peace Conference* by J T Shotwell (New York: 1937); Shotwell was a member of the US delegation. Count Albert Apponyi, the leader of the Hungarian delegation to the Conference, published memoirs of which part is devoted to Trianon: *The Memoirs of Count Apponyi* (London: 1935). There are valuable nuggets in *Essays on World War I: Total War and Peacemaking – A Case Study on Trianon*, edited by B K Királyi, P Pastor and I Sanders (New York: 1982).

Picture Sources

The author and publishers wish to express their thanks to the following sources of illustrative material and/or permission to reproduce it. They will make proper acknowledgements in future editions in the event that any omissions have occurred.

Getty Images: p. 52. Topham Picturepoint: pp. vi, x, 108.

Endpapers

The Signing of Peace in the Hall of Mirrors, Versailles, 28th June 1919 by Sir William Orpen (Imperial War Museum: akg Images)

Front row: Dr Johannes Bell (Germany) signing with Herr Hermann Müller leaning over him

Middle row (seated, left to right): General Tasker H Bliss, Col E M House, Mr Henry White, Mr Robert Lansing, President Woodrow Wilson (United States); M Georges Clemenceau (France); Mr David Lloyd George, Mr Andrew Bonar Law, Mr Arthur J Balfour, Viscount Milner, Mr G N Barnes (Great Britain); Prince Saionji (Japan)

Back row (left to right): M Eleftherios Venizelos (Greece);

Dr Afonso Costa (Portugal); Lord Riddell (British Press);
Sir George E Foster (Canada); M Nikola Pašić (Serbia);
M Stephen Pichon (France); Col Sir Maurice Hankey,
Mr Edwin S Montagu (Great Britain); the Maharajah of
Bikaner (India); Signor Vittorio Emanuele Orlando (Italy);
M Paul Hymans (Belgium); General Louis Botha (South
Africa); Mr W M Hughes (Australia)

Jacket images

(Front): Topham Picturepoint.
(Back): *Peace Conference at the Quai d'Orsay* by Sir William
Orpen (Imperial War Museum: akg Images).
Left to right (seated): Signor Orlando (Italy); Mr Robert
Lansing, President Woodrow Wilson (United States); M
Georges Clemenceau (France); Mr David Lloyd George, Mr
Andrew Bonar Law, Mr Arthur J Balfour (Great Britain);
Left to right (standing): M Paul Hymans (Belgium); Mr
Eleftherios Venizelos (Greece); The Emir Feisal (The
Hashemite Kingdom); Mr W F Massey (New Zealand);
General Jan Smuts (South Africa); Col E M House (United
States); General Louis Botha (South Africa); Prince Saionji
(Japan); Mr W M Hughes (Australia); Sir Robert Borden
(Canada); Mr G N Barnes (Great Britain); M Ignacy
Paderewski (Poland)

Index

A

Apponyi, Count Albert
92–9, 101, 104–6, 115
Ashmead-Bartlett, Ellis 56,
81
Austria 4, 8–10, 26, 27,
31–2, 43, 44, 46, 75–6, 82,
91, 95, 96, 113, 115–17,
124, 132

B

Balfour, Arthur 74
Bandholtz, General Harry
Hill 84, 86, 88–9
Bánffy, Miklós 98, 99, 116
Belá IV, King 4
Benárd, Ágoston 106
Beneš, Eduard 47, 49, 71,
85
Berinkey, Dénes 38, 41, 59
Berthelot, Philippe 101

Bethlen, István
Anti-Bolshevik
Committee, leads 81–3
anti-Semitic laws,
opposition to 131,
132–3, 134
death 137–9
early life 20–1
escapes Kun regime 65
political career pre-1914
21–3
prime minister, as 115–17
dismissal 126–7
revision of treaty terms,
and 120–5, 128–30
Beveridge, William 40
Böhm, Vilmos 59–60, 77
Bolsheviks 30, 56, 61, 64, 70
Bonsal, Stephen 56
Brailsford, H N 63
Bratianu, Ion 70, 73, 86

Brusilov, General 23
Bryce, Viscount 100
Bulgaria 23, 96

C

Charles IV, Emperor 25, 27,
    32–3, 34, 113
    attempts to reclaim
        crown 115–16
Charpé, General 83
Clemenceau, Georges 36,
    39, 58, 72, 82, 94–8
Clerk, Sir George 85–7,
    89–90
Csáky, Imre 103, 106
Cunninghame, Colonel 40,
    42, 81, 83
Curzon, Lord 100, 102
Czechoslovakia 70, 71, 75,
    77, 82, 101, 105, 113,
    133
Czernin, Count 25

D

Deák, Ferenc 7, 9
Drasche-Lázár, Alfred 106

F

First World War, the 13–14,
    22–30, 31–9
Foch, Marshal Ferdinand
    58, 78

Fourteen Points, the 26,
    28–9, 38, 58
France 16, 27, 39, 40, 49,
    103, 123
Franchet d'Esperey, General
    35–6, 58
Franz Ferdinand, Archduke
    13, 25
Franz Josef, Emperor 9, 13,
    23, 24, 94, 114

G

Garbai, Sándor 62
Germany 12–13, 16, 19,
    23, 27, 35, 43, 44, 72,
    74, 76, 80, 91, 96, 114,
    123, 125, 131–2, 135–6,
    142
Gömbös, Gyula 124, 126,
    131–2
Göring, Hermann 131
Gorton, General 84
Great Britain 39, 49, 67,
    123, 136

H

Hitler, Adolf 79, 133, 135,
    137, 142
Hohenlohe, Princess
    Stefania 124
Horthy, Admiral Miklós
    87–90, 99, 106, 113,

114–15, 117, 126–7, 128,
131, 132–3, 135–8, 142
Hungary
  anti-Semitism 80, 88,
    115, 126, 131–2, 134–5
  armed forces 36, 76–8,
    124, 136
  armistice terms 35–6
  Austrian rule, and 5–6,
    7–11
  Communist takeover
    138–40
  early history 3–5
  First World War, and
    13–16, 23–30
  Germany, and 12–13, 16,
    19, 43, 80, 123, 125,
    131–6, 142
  Italy, and 45, 123–5, 131,
    133–4
  Kun regime 56–65
  monarchy, fall of 31–4
  nationalities issue 6–7,
    11–13, 22–30, 34–5,
    45–9, 67–72, 93, 95,
    104–5, 128–9, 141–3
  'Red Army' 76–8
  revision of treaty terms
    111–13, 115–17,
    124–5, 128–30, 131–4
  Romanian occupation
    73–80, 83–9

Second World War, and
  135–9
treaty terms, and 67–75,
  95–106
Vienna Awards, the
  133–6, 140, 142
Huszár, Károlyi 89

I
Italy 34, 39, 45, 91, 95, 123,
  124, 125, 131, 133–4

J
Japan 39, 74, 95
Jászi, Oszkár 35
Josef, Archduke 30, 32–4,
  85
Joseph II, Emperor 6

K
Kállay, Miklós 137
Károlyi, Gyula 83, 87, 93,
  131
Károlyi, Mihály
  armistice, and 37–40
  death 140
  early life 17–18
  exile 63, 139
  government 33–4, 55,
    58–62
  land reform, and 41–2
  nationalities, and 27–8

opposition to First World
War 25–6
parliamentary career
19–20, 23
return to Hungary 140
Károlyi, Sandor 18, 21
Kossuth, Lajos 9 7, 9, 19, 20
Krudy, Gyula 41
Kun, Béla 37, 56–7, 60–1,
62–4, 72–3, 77–80, 82

L
Lakatos-Kállay, General 138
Landler, Jenő 61
Lansing, Robert 48, 74
Leeper, Allen 67–8, 101–2
Lenin, Vladimir 57, 64, 65
Lloyd George, David 39, 45,
72–3, 95, 97–8, 100, 102
London, Treaty of (1915) 45
Louis II, King 4

M
Maclean, Sir Donald 100
Maisky, Ivan 139
Maria Theresa, Empress 6,
20
Marie of Romania, Queen
86
Masaryk, Jan 140
Masaryk, Tomáš 46–7, 49
Mensdorff, Count 44

Millerand, Alexandre 98,
101, 104–5, 106, 120
Mindszenty, Cardinal 140
Münnich, Ferenc 37
Mussolini, Benito 123–4

N
Nagy, Ferenc 140
Naumann, Friedrich 43
Newton, Lord 100
Nicholas I, Tsar 9
Nicholson, Harold 67–8, 70
Nitti, Francesco 96, 101

O
Orlando, Vittorio 39

P
Paléologue, Maurice 102–3
Paris Peace Conference, the
43–50, 67–76, 84, 91–106
Hungarian delegation
91–4
Pašić, Nikola 46, 49
Peidl, Gyula 79, 83, 84
Petőfi, Sándor 111

R
Rákóczi, Ferenc 5
Rákosi, Mátyás 37, 139,
140, 141
Renner, Karl 82

Romania 22–4, 27, 37, 45, 49, 58–9, 70–1, 75, 83–5, 101, 105, 113, 143
  occupation of Hungary 74–5, 77–9, 83–8
Rothermere, Lord 124–5
Russia 13, 16, 30, 37, 44, 61, 62, 64–5, 82, 130, 135

S
Schnetzer, General 88
Second World War, the 135–8
Seton-Watson, Robert 47–8, 68, 70
Sigismund I 4
Simonyi, Henrik 61–2
Sixtus, Prince 27
Smuts, Jan 44, 73
St Germain, Treaty of 91
Steed, Wickham 47, 68
Stephen I, King 3
Stromfeld, Aurél 77, 78
Supilo, Frano 46
Sylvester II, Pope 3
Számuely, Tibor 37, 65, 79
Szántó, Béla 57
Széchenyi, Andor 127
Széchenyi, István 7–8, 20
Széchenyi, Countess 'Minci' 126–7

T
Teleki, Count Pál 92, 93, 97, 99, 106, 113, 115, 135, 136
Tisza, István 12, 19, 22, 23, 25, 26, 31, 32, 43, 63, 75, 94, 120
Tisza, Kálmán 10, 12, 120
Trianon, Treaty of 75–6, 113, 115–16, 129, 134, 141
Trumbić, Ante 46, 49

U
United States of America 21, 40, 48–9, 69–70, 74, 84, 91, 94, 96

V
Versailles, Treaty of 76, 91, 99
Vyx, Lt-Col. Fernand 37, 42, 59, 60, 61, 62, 65, 73

W
Wall Street Crash, the 126
Wallace, Henry 96
Wilhelm II, Kaiser 12, 23
Wilson, Woodrow 26, 38–9, 44, 48, 55, 56, 72–3, 91, 97